DAD'S EVERYTHING BOOK
FOR SONS

Other Books in This Series

Dad's Everything Book for Daughters
by John Trent, Ph.D.

Mom's Everything Book for Sons
by Becky Freeman

Mom's Everything Book for Daughters
by Becky Freeman

DAD'S EVERYTHING BOOK
FOR SONS

• practical ideas for a quality relationship •

JOHN TRENT, PH.D.
AND GREG JOHNSON

WOMEN OF FAITH℠

ZONDERVAN™

GRAND RAPIDS, MICHIGAN 49530 USA

We want to hear from you. Please send your comments about this book to us in care of zreview@zondervan.com. Thank you.

GRAND RAPIDS, MICHIGAN 49530 USA

WWW.ZONDERVAN.COM

Dad's Everything Book for Sons
Copyright © 2003 by John Trent, Greg Johnson, and Women of Faith, Inc.

Requests for information should be addressed to:
Zondervan, *Grand Rapids, Michigan 49530*

Library of Congress Cataloging-in-Publication Data

Trent, John T.
  Dad's everything book for sons : practical ideas for a quality relationship / John Trent, Greg Johnson.
      p. cm.
  ISBN 0-310-24293-2
  1. Fathers and sons—Religious aspects—Christianity. I. Johnson, Greg, 1956– II. Title.
  BV4529.17 .T74 2003
  248.8'421–dc21

                                                                          2002156149

Published in association with the literary agency of Alive Communications, Inc., 7680 Goddard Street, Suite 200, Colorado Springs, CO 80920.

Interior design by Todd Sprague

Printed in the United States of America

03 04 05 06 07 08 09/❖ DC/ 10 9 8 7 6 5 4 3 2 1

To my now grown sons, Troy and Drew
You are the continual light of my life
I love being your dad and am grateful to God
for the privilege of being part of the process
as you head toward Christian manhood
—Greg Johnson

Contents

A Brief Introduction
by John Trent

The first thing you should know is that I have daughters. Two of the cutest a dad could ask for. My writing compatriot here, Greg Johnson, has two sons. He tells me they used to be cute, but since they're both out of high school now, that description would get him into big trouble. He asked me to collaborate on this book (though I really didn't contribute all that much) because of one big reason: my personality profile. You see, after navigating his boys through childhood and their teenage years, he told me he is absolutely evangelistic in his belief that recognizing each son's personality and strengths is the key to being a great dad.

Did you ever have a coach who treated every player alike? Each team member got the same browbeating scowl. They'd also get similar long looks of disgust when they messed up on the field or the court. And over the course of the year, that coach would make sure every young athlete got the tongue-lashing he deserved. I was a wrestler in high school and Coach Curtis was the exact opposite. Though, judging by his background, you never would have thought it. He was a wrestler in college—a good one—and fought in the Korean conflict. If you saw the movie *Pork Chop Hill*, you might have seen a composite of Coach. He was an army ranger and one tough hombre.

I was a wrestler on his team for four years. He had this challenge he gave to every wrestler in every weight class. He'd get down on all fours, put his left hand behind his back, and then one by one we'd get down in the wrestling position and try to move his right arm off the mat. If we could move or lift it in any way, we could skip practice.

In four years not one wrestler in any weight class could get his arm off the mat.

Tough hombre.

It was my freshman year and I was just a skinny kid. The varsity wrestler in my weight class was hurt, so at the end of the year I had to compete in the conference championships (after winning just one match all year). Well, needless to say, I was overmatched. By the time it was over, the score was twenty-two to two. I walked off the mat dejected, hanging my head. Coach Curtis ran over to me, put his arm around me, and said, "Well, John, at least you didn't get pinned!"

I looked up at him and could see that he meant what he said. Not getting pinned was a huge victory for me; I just didn't realize it. At the right moment he knew exactly what I needed.

And that's the role of a dad in one simple sentence: Know your kids well enough to know exactly what they need, when they need it.

The best coaches are students of their players and find ways to individually motivate them to get the best out of them. And that's what dads have to do for their sons.

You may have a boy who's destined to be a "dumb jock," and another who's a dreamer. If you treat them both the same in how you discipline, how you talk to them about life and faith, and especially how you try to build a solid relationship with them before they arrive at their teenage years, then you're likely heading for some trouble—or, as Greg calls it, "the approaching waterfall."

I'm going to come back in a chapter or two to talk about how to assess your son's personality by using a simple test that will actually be something fun you can do together. I'll also be back a few more times throughout the book, but for now I'm going to place you squarely into Greg's capable hands as he offers stories and ideas about how to take your relationship with your son to places you never thought possible. If by the time you finish this book, you don't feel more than ready to enjoy and persevere through your son's teenage years, well, you were watching too much *SportsCenter* while trying to read it.

How to Use This Book

Thanks, John! Nice handoff. You've picked up this book because you have a son in the eight- to twelve-year-old range. And if your wife bought this book for you and told you to read it, well, you could do worse things with your time than thumb through these pages. Our whole intent in writing this small book was to pack it full of ideas to help you accomplish the goal of having your son come to know and follow Jesus Christ, while at the same time making your relationship with your boy the best it can possibly be.

I wish I could say I tried half the suggestions in this book, but I can't. That's the bad news. The good news is, my sons are turning out pretty good despite my imperfection. But many sons don't turn out that good.

In most books the author wants you to walk away doing at least one thing that will move you farther along the path of the Christian life, marriage, parenting, and so forth. This book wants to give you dozens of ideas to put into practice in the next five years. To help you accomplish this goal, on the next page we've given you room to write down the ideas you want to implement. I'm a guy, so I know that unless you write down some sort of plan or strategy, the best ideas in this book that apply to you and your son may remain ideas, not action.

So be a man of action and grab a pencil while you're reading this book. Take a few notes, then employ as many of these suggestions as you can. Why? Because as John hinted a few pages ago, there's some fast-moving water in the distance. Can you hear what's ahead?

My "Don't Forget" List

1. Ideas I Need to Implement Right Away

2. Ideas I Need to Implement in the Next Year

3. Ideas I Don't Want to Forget When the Teen Years Hit

Part One:

Building the Relationship

1. The Waterfall Approaches

While few dads would describe the preschool and early school years as a quiet canoe trip down a tranquil river, believe it or not, the water hasn't even begun to get choppy. And while some parents manage to raise perfect kids who help them paddle down the lazy river of mom- and dad-hood (that is, they got extremely lucky because God gave them compliant children), most seasoned parents aren't bashful about describing their son's teenage years as thundering rapids. And they, the parents, are stuck in the back of the boat, holding the rudder to keep the nose of the boat pointed in the right direction, mainly hanging on for dear life.

Do you hear the Niagara Falls–like waterfall in the distance? Some good friends of mine didn't.

Jason, their oldest son, was handsome, athletically gifted, a great student, and knew how to charm a rich uncle out of his wallet. And spiritual? No one could memorize verses at AWANA the way Jason could. By age thirteen, however, his growth spurt hadn't hit. That left him odd man out at gym basketball. He got picked with the nerds and smokers. Guess who his friends started to become? Since the nerds weren't cool, he picked the smokers. Smokers, as we all remember from our teenage years, usually became the drinkers, then the stoners, then the drop-out-of-school-because-it's-so-uncoolers. Read: every parent's nightmare.

By age eighteen Jason was taking heroin. At age twenty he was in and out of rehab. He hit bottom by joining the ranks of the homeless at Union Gospel Mission shelters throughout the Rocky Mountain region.

Okay, let's push stop on this video from the pit of hades and realize one thing: your cute grade school son whose voice is set to change in the not-too-distant future likely won't be on heroin before the end of the decade. Maybe he won't rebel at all ... not even a little. But maybe you're in dreamland about what lies ahead. It's tough raising a teenage son. No, *real* tough.

That's why these years between eight and twelve are perhaps the most important years of your parenting career. You have at least four years to solidify the relationship for life. When your son's a teenager, he'll be busy breaking away, getting ready for adulthood, and basically trying to pretend in public he doesn't know you. Fine. Good. You want to let him go and be a living, breathing adult, clothed and in his right mind. But when you let adolescents go—or when they let you go—sometimes they crash ... hard.

The safety net your son needs, and the reason God is keeping you around, is to be there when he comes back. What will bring him back from a short walk down that prodigal road—or a long prodigal marathon over the mountains and canyons he's put between himself and you (or between himself and God)—is your relationship with him.

A Sure-fire Formula?

Since my own faith journey didn't include growing up in a Christian home—and since I remember *very well* what my journey was like—I've been determined to raise my two boys in a way in which God's love could always be within their reach. That means taking them to church, Sunday school, AWANA, having one-on-one devotions with them ... whatever. My goal has been to have them know Christ early in life and grow from there.

About ten years ago I thought it would be educational and enlightening to interview parents who had raised children who stuck with the faith, and then interview the adult children who had been raised by these faithful parents. My hope was that I'd discover the habits and attitudes necessary to make sure I did it right. (Actually, I was looking for the magic formula to *guarantee* that my boys would stick with God—if one existed.)

My writing partner and I surveyed hundreds of parents and adult children (over age twenty-one), then followed up the surveys with dozens of phone interviews. The results were fascinating.

One-third of our sampling of adult children who had "made it" had gone through full-blown rebellion. That is, they left the church—and the Lord—for an extended period of time before coming back. Another one-third had "rebellious times" but always stayed in church. The final third never drifted far from the Lord.

My question was obvious: "What made the two-thirds of adult children come back to the faith they had—at various times and in various ways—tried to escape?"

We found out that parents generally had three ways they tried to impart spiritual truth: (1) emphasizing behavior, (2) emphasizing content (biblical truth), or (3) emphasizing the relationship.

If you took these three factors and made them three rings of a target, what would be your bull's-eye? What would your son say was your bull's-eye? Bigger question: What's God's bull's-eye?

An accurate read of the Bible would indicate that all three are important to a growing, active faith. But only one thing is the bull's-eye, both between God and us and between you and your soon-to-be teenager: the relationship. Jesus didn't have to die because we didn't know the Bible. And he didn't just die because our behavior wasn't appropriate. He died because our sinful nature had caused our hearts to bend away from God. Where our hearts went, our behavior followed. He died to restore a right relationship between God and us.

Guess what the one-third of adult children who said they went into full-blown rebellion *perceived* their parent's bull's-eye to be? If you chose behavior, you win a cookie. Conversely, the ones who stuck with the faith said they had a great relationship with their parents. With few exceptions, those who came back to the faith could trace their epiphany to a renewed relationship with their now older parent. The reconciliation stories I heard were tearjerkers. It was amazing to see that when the parent-child relationship was healed, the relationship with God often followed.

What's your bull's-eye with your son?

While most dads would say it's the relationship, many are unknowingly implying, by their words and actions, that good behavior and right beliefs hold the key to Dad's love and acceptance. A child will naturally conclude that this is what God is mainly concerned about too. It's not hard to walk away from a God who only cares about boring theology and towing the line.

There is certainly a time and a place where behavior and spiritual content must be emphasized. We don't do our boys any favors if we let them run amuck, and right beliefs about God's character and his plan for salvation have to be made clear. But if both are not seasoned with heavy doses of hugs, time, and consistent unconditional love, the challenge to better behavior and right beliefs will fall on deaf ears.

It's not spiritual content.

It's not just behavior.

Those two circles on the target are important but they're not the bull's-eye. Relationship is.

That's what this book is about. It's designed to give you tons of ideas about how to creatively—yet with purpose behind the fun and the serious—give your son a relationship he can enjoy today and know he can always come back to. No matter what mistake he's made, no matter how many miles he seems away from you and God, he will always need a place to return to.

Relationship is the key for you and God too, isn't it? It's not just content from God's Word; it's not just you knowing right from wrong and doing the right; it's that Jesus Christ died to give you open access to a God of grace and mercy. God is someone whose arms you can always fall into when nothing else in life is working. He's someone you can *always* come back to.

A human representative of God on planet Earth is what you're supposed to be to your son, but it doesn't just happen by accident. It has to be intentional.

If your goal is to give your son everything he needs to face adulthood and a lifetime of walking with the Savior, this book will help. But before we get completely started, you need to understand what type of hand you've been dealt in terms of how God has uniquely put your son together. All sons are not created equal. And since you're a motivated dad who wants to do the best by each son he's been entrusted with, you have to adjust your dad style to the individual nature of your son.

2. His Unique Personality

As promised, this is John and I'm back again. How do I know that not all boys—not even all brothers—are created equal? I have a twin brother named Jeff. Though we look very much alike, he and I are very different in personality and God-given strengths. My two daughters, Kari and Laura, also look very much alike, yet they're in different time zones when it comes to their God-given strengths. Dad, if you're serious about connecting with your son, it's important to understand his unique, personal, and God-given personality and strengths. I want to show you a quick way to get a firm grasp on it all. What follows is called the LOGB Personal Strengths Survey. It's a short test I created to assess strengths, and it can help you quickly discover not only your son's unique, God-given strengths but yours as well.

This is an instrument you want to take with you during a father-son fun time with your eight- to twelve-year-old. Here's how you get started: First, you have permission to photocopy this assessment for you and your son. Run off four copies, as you'll need two surveys each. I'll explain why shortly. This is a "first guess" assessment, meaning you should try to take this assessment in three minutes or less. (Believe it or not, that's more than enough time for most people. If you're married, your spouse could fill this out on you in thirty seconds, so don't agonize for hours over words. First response!)

After you've photocopied the survey, you'll see there are four boxes. Starting with the L box, circle each word that describes who you tend to be as a person. You're looking at how you tend to act overall, not just as a father. For example, do you tend to be fairly assertive as a person? If so, circle the word *assertive* in the L box. Do you tend to take charge? If so, circle those words. Circle every word or phrase that describes who you are in the L box, and the statement at the bottom if it applies to you. (The statement in the L box is, "Let's do it now!")

In summary, there are fourteen words and phrases and one statement in the L box. Circle each of these that describes you. When you're finished, add up the number of items circled, double the number, and write your score in the space provided. So, for example, if you circled six words and phrases and the statement "Let's do it now," that's seven circles. Seven doubled equals fourteen, which is your score for the L box.

Here's what you do with that score. The Personal Strengths Survey Chart below the assessment consists of a graph that ranges from zero to thirty, with a midline at fifteen. If your score in the L box was fourteen, on the L scale you'd put a dot just under the midline, approximately where fourteen would be. (See the example.) Once you've transferred your score to the graph, go on to the O, G, and B boxes, repeating the above process. That is, for each box circle every word, phrase, and statement that describes you, double the number of items circled, write down your score, and then plot your score on the graph.

Finally, connect the dots on the LOGB scales and you have a diagram—and a way to quickly see which is your highest and lowest score. (Many people have scores in two or more boxes that tie or are very close, which is perfectly acceptable. For example, someone may score fairly close on the L and O scales, or on the G and B scales.)

After you've completed your strengths assessment, get your son to fill out his. If he struggles with some of the words, you can help him, but let him circle all the words himself as much as possible. Next, using the two extra copies of the survey, have him assess your strengths while you assess his. You'll each start with how you look at yourselves, but it's very helpful and informative for you to see how your son looks at you, and for him to see what strengths you observe in him.

I've written an entire book about this LOGB assessment with my good friend Gary Smalley, called *The Two Sides of Love*. But in brief summary here's what the LOGB scales illustrate:

If you or your son scored highest on the L scale, that means you're a "Lion." Lions are take-charge, strong, assertive people. At work they tend to be the boss (or at least they think they are!). They're so decisive, they can be impatient if obstacles block their way, which is why most Lions think stoplights are a tool of Satan! They like to keep the car moving and keep moving toward their goals. They're great leaders but sometimes they need to be better listeners. That's a picture of the Lions.

Then you have the O's, or "Otters." Otters are fun-loving and very verbal people. They love to yak, yak, yak! They have lots of friends and acquaintances and like change and "new" things. They tend to be very creative and may not be well organized. They're the ones with the sock *room*, not the sock drawer! When they grow up, they don't balance the checkbook; they just switch banks. They're fun people but sometimes need to be more serious or organized to get more done.

The people who score highest in the G scale are the "Golden Retrievers." They're great team players and are steady and understanding and want everyone to feel close and

Personal Strengths Survey

L

Takes charge	Bold
Determined	Purposeful
Assertive	Decision maker
Firm	Leader
Enterprising	Goal-driven
Competitive	Self-reliant
Enjoys challenges	Adventurous

"Let's do it now!"

Double the number circled _____

O

Takes risks	Fun-loving
Visionary	Likes variety
Motivator	Enjoys change
Energetic	Creative
Very verbal	Group-oriented
Promoter	Mixes easily
Avoids details	Optimistic

"Trust me! It'll work out!"

Double the number circled _____

G

Loyal	Adaptable
Nondemanding	Sympathetic
Even keel	Thoughtful
Avoids conflict	Nurturing
Enjoys routine	Patient
Dislikes change	Tolerant
Deep relationships	Good Listener

"Let's keep things
the way they are."

Double the number circled _____

B

Deliberate	Discerning
Controlled	Detailed
Reserved	Analytical
Predictable	Inquisitive
Practical	Precise
Orderly	Persistent
Factual	Scheduled

"How was it done
in the past?"

Double the number circled _____

Personal Strengths Survey Chart

	L	O	G	B
30				
15				
0				

connected in the family. They're very compassionate. For example, they tend to buy twenty boxes of Girl Scout cookies every year because it's so hard to say no! On the positive side, they're great listeners and are soft with people. However, sometimes they're too soft on problems.

Finally, you have those dads and sons who score highest on the B scale. These are the "Beavers," who are detailed, organized, and precise. They like to finish things they start. (Otters like to start things . . . and more things . . . and several more things!) Beavers are very good at detail projects and find comfort in a systematic or specific, spelled-out way of doing things. They're very good at taking things apart, but sometimes they can be very hard on themselves or critical of others because of their high standards.

Now that you and your son have finished your surveys, take a long meal or a short drive to talk about each other's strengths. This is a great way for you to highlight some of his strengths that you see (the things you circled in your assessment of him) and to praise him for them. (Each word he circled in his assessment of himself can be a strength he sees in himself. If you see other words he didn't circle that represent traits he demonstrates, point those out as well.)

As you talk about his strengths and help him to see your own, this may be a good time to ask some informational questions about your relationship. For example, let's say your son ranked you high on the Lion scale, yet you scored yourself much higher on the Otter scale. Talk about that difference in perspective. If he's looking at you as a roaring Lion when you see yourself as a playful, encouraging Otter, ask him for an example or two to explain why he views you that way. Don't be defensive, but realize that you're getting tremendous feedback as to how he really sees you. For example, I scored myself high as an Otter, but Laura, my younger daughter, scored me higher as a Lion. When I asked her why, she said, "I see you being more of an Otter with other people. But at home, particularly when you're tired, I think you are a lot more of a Lion." Ouch! Yet that honest feedback led to some very positive discussions ... and a commitment to include more fun times with Laura (and more sleep so Mr. Grumpy didn't come out!).

I (Greg) love these four little animals because they are generally right on when it comes to describing people. On rare occasion is someone dominantly just one type. Most of us have various percentages of each. If I were to describe myself, I'd be forty percent Golden Retriever, thirty percent Beaver, twenty percent Otter, and ten percent Lion. I'm a people person who is pretty organized, but I like to have fun (and make sure others are having fun too). How long have I been this way? Probably since I was born.

My wife, Elaine, on the other hand, is fifty percent Beaver and then an even percentage of the other three. She likes to keep things organized ... and she ended up being an office manager and bookkeeper. She does who she is.

Our oldest son, Troy, is exactly like her, and our youngest son, Drew, is nearly exactly like me. It's very weird how this turned out. And they've been this way since they were little!

I wanted John to give us his input on these personality types because it's essential for you to understand how God has wired your son. If you don't recognize these general traits in him, you may not become a perceptive dad who goes with the flow of the bents of his son. You may wind up forcing a square peg into a round hole. What this does is alienate your child. And this is the last thing you want to do as a parent. As I said earlier, relationship is everything in the big picture of raising your son.

Did your dad treat you and your siblings all the same? I have a coaching story that, like John's example in the preceding pages, illustrates the importance of knowing each family member.

I had one of the best high school basketball coaches in the state of Oregon. One reason why he was so successful was that he knew how to handle each of his players differently to get their maximum performance. He knew that I was a bit more sensitive, so he rarely yelled at me. He'd take me aside after practice and help me see areas of my game where I needed to improve. I would have run through a wall for this man. My baseball coach, however, chewed me out in front of everyone during one game because I got picked off of first when a guy missed a bunt. I drove to his house the next day and put my uniform on his doorstep. His intention, I believe, wasn't to get me to quit, but his tactics gave me no other option.

If you have one son or multiple children, you must take into account each child's individual propensities as you seek to be the best dad you can be. The Bible makes one strong admonition specifically to fathers about their parenting style: "Fathers, do not embitter your children, or they will become discouraged" (Colossians 3:21). Other translations use the word *exasperate.* How do we embitter or exasperate our sons? By not recognizing their personality type, their natural inclinations, and how God has gifted them. We have to treat each son as an individual and go with the flow of who God made them to be.

Dads: If this short assessment has whetted your appetite for understanding both your son's strengths and your own, here's a challenge: For almost two years I worked alongside several outstanding experts in online assessment to create what's called the Ministry Insights Report. It allows you to go online, fill out a short survey, and then instantly receive an email containing a twenty-eight-page online strengths assessment. That's twenty-eight pages of reliable information on a son as young as eight (if you help him with certain vocabulary), and, if you do a survey on yourself, for your son to learn more about you.

My wife, Cindy, and I used this tool to assess ourselves and had both our daughters do the same. It turned into one of the best family night activities we have ever pursued. There is a cost for the assessment, yet it's reasonable and, I feel, well worth the expense. To order the report or to obtain more information about it, just visit us at www.strongfamilies.com and you'll see an icon with the four animals—the Lion, Otter, Golden Retriever, and Beaver. Click on that icon and you'll find out more about this extremely accurate, informative tool for ministry, workplace, and family teams—like dad-son teams!

3. Get Him Talking

One of your primary goals is to get your son talking. Not easy with men, not easy with boys. Whether you're a talker yourself or you're the strong, silent type, you must— I repeat, *must*—get your young son used to conversing in normal ways. How?

1. Find his talking place.
2. Develop a "moon talk" code.

Let me pick off these two essentials one at a time.

Find His Talking Place

I do not know of any boy who won't talk with his dad if he's in the right place at the right time. The key is finding that right "talking place." I had to do a lot of experimenting before I found the right talking place with my sons. And I learned that after a couple of years it usually changes. The ideas below should help you discover your son's talking place (now and as it evolves over the years) and get the conversation flowing.

Your goal is twofold: (1) make it easy for him, and (2) keep your expectations low.

His Favorite Ball

I could discuss almost anything with one of my sons while we were together doing something with a ball, whether it was playing catch with a baseball or football, shooting hoops, or kicking a soccer ball back and forth. And while the goal wasn't always to turn that fifteen to thirty minutes into a sermon or counseling opportunity, I learned that I didn't want to miss out on the chance to get him talking, either. All I did was try to think about one question I wanted to ask. If I had more than one, I started with easy questions first to get him in the rhythm of talking. Questions like:

> "What's the best thing about school these days? The worst?"
> "Who's your best friend now? Why?"
> "Is there anything about Mom that bugs you?"
> "Have I done anything lately that has made you mad?"
> "If you could do anything this summer, what would it be?"
> "What would your dream vacation be like?"
> "How do you like spending time with . . . ?" (Name a grandparent or some other relative he's close to.)
> "What do you think you're really good at?"
> "What would you like to be good at?"
> "What if . . . ?" (Play a one-sentence version of the what-if game. I'm pretty much a what-if fanatic with boys, so I've included some longer what-if situations toward the back of the book for you to do together with your son. These are just some samples of the types of things you can cover. The one-sentence variety should be easy for you to think up.)

Naturally, you have to adjust your questions based on your son's age and maturity level. And you start with some easy yes or no questions for him to answer. Two last things:

(1) silence is okay, and (2) don't make any time predictable (try not to let him suspect that you're using fun things with him to get him talking).

Hot Tub (If You Have One)

This was my oldest son's talking place for several years. I think seeing me without a shirt on made me less of a threat. (No comments from the cheap seats.) As he hit his teenage years, this was the place where he would open up about girls, sports rivalries with other guys at school, and other things personal. I'm sure he didn't tell me everything, but I was amazed at what he *would* open up about. For those three or four years I told everyone I knew that the hot tub was the best investment in our relationship that I ever made.

The Car

My youngest son's talking place was the car. When kids are between the ages of eight and twelve, they're usually not pushing every button on the radio dial trying to find their favorite song. So if you're not addicted to music or talk radio yourself, the car may be the perfect place to get him heading in the right direction, practicing his communication skills so his future wife won't blame you for raising a son with the personality of a post.

Other Ideas

For your son it might be walks through the woods as you're going to your favorite hunting spot or fishing hole. Maybe it will be over dessert at Denny's or along the trek to obtain Krispy Kremes (um, for Mom, of course). Whatever, get creative until you find it . . . then milk it for all it's worth to get him talking about deeper stuff. He needs to see that you are a good listener, that you'll hold things in confidence (not tell Mom everything), and that you occasionally (and sparingly) have a few pearls of wisdom. Most boys want to figure some things out on their own. They don't like being told what to do, think, and feel about everything. If your son senses this happening, he'll clam up.

Develop a "Moon Talk" Code

Years ago when the Tom Hanks movie *Apollo 13* came out, I took my two sons, plunked down way too much money for tickets—and prayed they wouldn't get hungry. Fortunately, the movie had them chewing on their nails instead of buckets of popcorn. When it came out on video, we bought it the first day of its release. Why? The film was mostly clean, had great acting, and moved my emotions, but most importantly the flick was filled with great illustrations.

As a diligent dad, I'm always looking for teachable moments with my two boys. And if I can point to something *they* can relate to, the lesson sinks in better.

A couple weeks after watching the video for the tenth time, it hit me: the crew safely reached their destination not because everything went perfectly; they made it back to earth through a series of mistakes . . . and midcourse corrections that put them back on course.

Sounded like real life to me, so I tried something. I took my oldest on a "date" to McDonald's, and between bites we talked about the movie. "Even though everything seemed to go wrong," my son said, "they still made it home. Good thing the crew had Gene Kranz back in Houston to keep all the rescue efforts on track."

I saw the opening I was looking for.

"Son, can I make a point about what I see is a good message from this movie?" (If I ask his permission to sermonize, he'll usually say yes.)

"Sure, Dad."

"Troy, your goal in life is to complete your mission. I don't know what that is yet and neither do you. But along the way a lot of things are going to go wrong. Some *sorta* wrong and some *really* wrong. Hitting problems, however, isn't the issue. It's getting back on course. Right?"

"Right."

"Though your life—your mission—isn't something I want to control, God has given me the responsibility to help when midcourse corrections are needed. Do you agree that's a role I ought to play?"

"Sometimes."

"That's right, *sometimes.* A lot of times you'll need to figure things out on your own. Like when the crew realized they needed to move from the command module to the LEM. They didn't need Houston to tell them they would run out of oxygen.

"What I'd like to do is occasionally have what I'll call a 'moon talk.' It will be a time when I think a midcourse correction is necessary. I promise they won't be weekly occurrences, maybe not even monthly, but when I ask you if we can have a moon talk, I want you to take it extra seriously. No rolling your eyes or trying to find something else to do. Does this sound like something you can agree to?"

"As long as it's not too often. I'm almost a teenager now, so I can figure most things out for myself."

Fighting the urge to laugh out loud, I nodded my head. Since that day we've had several moon talks, regarding subjects such as:

- how his treatment of his mother would be the number one key I would look to as he wanted to spend more time with females
- secular media intake
- sex (this one more than once)
- his temper and how he behaved on the basketball court
- how God is an even better Gene Kranz than I am

How about you? Have you found a way to obtain a listening, motivated ear when it's time to talk about the most important things in life? Or have you taken the easy way out by simply sermonizing—or raising your voice—whenever your son acts up or gets on your nerves?

It is most definitely your mission in life to be the Gene Kranz for your son. You must be proactive as he heads toward the teenage years and later out of your direct control. He needs to have the wisdom and skills to make his own midcourse corrections when you're not around. Develop your own code for when you need to have serious talks with your son, something he can readily identify, something unique to just you two. If you can't think of anything, watch *Apollo 13* together and try having your own moon talks. It may be a good place to start.

Progress Reports from Your Son

Permission to speak. Does your son have it with you? Or have you verbally or nonverbally told him that he's just a kid and his opinions are childish?

Secure fathers aren't afraid to hear the truth, no matter who in the family speaks it or through what immature filter it may arrive. Boys have opinions and their opinions matter. No, he doesn't know all the facts about everything. And no, he can't articulate his feelings about life as well as you can. But if you want a son who's not afraid to talk, he must be given permission to speak his mind . . . and not just about who's going to win this year's Super Bowl.

Are you creating an atmosphere in which nothing is out of bounds for discussion? If so, you and your son will enjoy a close relationship for a lifetime. But if he senses that certain subjects are taboo with dear old Dad, look forward to a measured relationship that will likely not make it to deeper levels.

Some dads are wired to keep things on the surface. I'm not. I want to know what my boys are thinking about everything, including me. So I've made it a habit to give them permission to speak their minds. Here are a few questions you should not be afraid to ask your son:

> "Is there any way I could be a better dad?"
> "Is there a way I could treat your brother or sister better?"
> "Could I treat your mom better somehow?"
> "If you could change one thing about me, what would it be?"

You get the point. These are the types of honest questions that on the surface might put me on the spot or somehow make my sons realize I'm not perfect. While you may think this could lower your son's view of you, the very opposite is true. If he sees you're vulnerable enough to ask him his opinion about something so personal as your performance, character, and decisions, he just might turn the tables. And this is what you want, isn't it? You have wisdom that life and God have taught you, and you want to share it. But unsolicited wisdom and advice, especially as your son gets older, will make him think that you're just trying to run his life. While a nickel's worth of free advice may sometimes be necessary, ideally you want him to ask for your opinion. Although it's a bad goal to want to run his life, it's a good goal to want him to have all the facts before he starts making important decisions.

By asking the types of questions above, you show your-self to be secure, humble, and someone who wants to improve his behavior to conform to the image of Christ. Do you show yourself to be insecure, proud, and a know-it-all dad if you don't ask? Well, yes, probably.

And this will be the type of son you'll raise. Someone who is too proud to ask advice or to be confronted with inconsistencies. This is the wrong message you want to send to your son as he's growing into a man. There are few things sadder than to see someone who acts as if he has it all together, when most everyone knows he doesn't. Healthy men are well acquainted with their faults. And while they don't want them paraded for the world to see, they give a few other men permission to tell them about anything they notice.

How do you teach this? By being a dad who gives his son permission to speak about things he might notice. This might be one of the biggest gifts you give your son: the ability to be vulnerable with another man. And the best way to give this gift is through your example.

Go ahead. Shock him today by asking his opinion on how you're doing as a dad. And then six months from now do it again. His pearls of wisdom won't fill a book, but that's not the point. The point is that he matters, his thoughts matter, and real men aren't afraid to invite other men into their inconsistencies. When "iron sharpens iron" (Proverbs 27:17), we best grow into the image of Christ.

The Answer Man

Do you love being the font of all knowledge about every-thing a boy needs to know? Does it make you feel that you're doing your job if you can point out areas about which your son is clueless?

If so, cut it out. You're not doing him any favors in preparing him for manhood. Boys need to struggle. They need to wrestle with questions. They rarely want to be told. They want to be valued. They need to learn the sense of God-reliance that is best learned by how they are fathered.

That doesn't mean you adopt a laissez-faire style of parenting and let your son do whatever comes to his immature, soon-to-be-hormone-driven brain. It means you learn the art of asking questions. (Do you see a theme reappearing?) Get him talking, get him thinking, and most importantly teach him to be a "noticer" when it comes to life. To do this, you must start young. Though he may be predisposed to becoming a "dumb jock," he can never know that from you. As far as you're concerned, he has a brain, he's perceptive, he makes good decisions, and he's good with people. How does he know this? Because you're telling him so.

> "Son, why do you think Sam is a better student than everyone else?"
>
> "Son, why is it that the teacher you don't like is always putting down kids in her class?"
>
> "Son, what do you think would happen if there were no police officers on the streets?"
>
> "Son, why do some people become missionaries to other countries, when living in America is easier? Do you think life is always about making choices that make your life easy?"

Again, you won't get answers like Dr. James Dobson's. But you will teach your son to think, that his opinions matter, and that he's growing up to be more than just a stud muffin for airheaded girls.

4. Defend Yourself Against Communication Killers

In that survey of parents and older children I conducted a number of years ago, I asked hundreds of adults to remember a number of significant things about their growing-up years. Among all the eye-opening info, I found that only about twenty percent of the participants communicated well with their parents. In fact, they said, "The teenage years were the worst."

What was the reason? Differences and *perceived* differences in values, brought on by—believe it or not—the media and a "generation gap."

Besides hiding your son away from the world, how can you prevent the influence of a sick society from entering your home? Like you, I've discovered that you can't protect your son from everything, so what I've tried to do is focus on things I can control. What do I want to control most? Interaction. That's why job one is to promote open communication with my boys *inside* the home, starting when they're young. (Are you hearing a pattern develop?) To do that, I have to be aware of what "communication killers" are lurking about. I found ten.

Communication Killer #1: Not Taking Time for Each Other

Remember what Jesus said one job of Satan is? "The thief comes only to steal and . . . destroy" (John 10:10). From the time children are very young, even in Christian families, the Dark One is allowed to steal and destroy the time that dads and sons spend together.

Here's the no-brainer of the day: *If you're not with someone, you can't communicate very well.*

I'm not a sociologist, but you don't have to be an expert to detect a trend. Families are chasing after the American dream, with split-level homes, two shiny cars in the garage, and the latest fashions. To afford all this stuff, Mom and Dad have to be *away* from the home earning money to pay for the goodies *inside* their home. And when the parents are home, they're often home only in body!

It's not a sin to live in a better neighborhood or drive a late-model car. But if nicer things are the goal, don't blame God, the church, or our culture when you can't communicate with your children or they've opted to stop going to church. The best way to invest in the future and plan for a happy retirement is to raise kids who follow the Lord with all their hearts.

In these days of unparalleled immorality, our kids need our time—from the day they are born until they leave the nest.

Examine your life and decide whether your relationship with your children could benefit from a few more hours a week. Then do something about it. You may have to do some radical rearranging. If so, do it soon.

Communication Killer #2: The Thing Everyone Stares At

The "one-eyed monster" deserves a trainload of blame for stifling communication between dads and sons. Sure, TV is an easy target to load, lock in, and fire on, but no one can deny its effect on families. Not only can it pump one-hundred-percent-pure filth into your home, but it can also rob literally months and years of valuable time away from talking, listening, and playing with your son—stuff that cements relationships for life.

True confession time: I own a TV set. Actually, I have three televisions hooked up to a cable system (but no premium channels). Do I make poor viewing choices? Sometimes, without a doubt. But I've discovered that families *can* have a balance and can even use TV to enhance family togetherness. TV sports have definitely allowed my two boys and me to enjoy bonding times. And when my boys were in grade school, I'd organize an "Ernest Film Festival." (More on that later.)

If the TV hurt our home in any way, it was probably that it caused me to *not* think about more creative times of communication we could have as a family. It did numb me a bit to initiating talks with my boys.

Communication Killer #3: Little Children Sometimes Grow into Obnoxious Teenagers

Three things are inevitable as kids grow up:

- puberty
- peer groups
- pop culture

Since we can't prevent puberty, protecting kids from the next two is tempting. But really, do we want to overprotect them forever or, as Mark Twain once suggested, lock them in a barrel and feed them through a hole?

How realistic is it to try to insulate them from every negative influence out there, be it a billboard or a friend who's into heavy metal music? Not very. A better strategy is to teach them discernment skills from their early years.

Some boys are more susceptible to peer group pressure and being influenced by the popular media's myth of "coolness." No, it's not genetic; it's a learned insecurity. Sometimes it's brought on through unstable grade school years during which one or both parents are uninvolved (time constraints, divorce, or fatigue). Often other circumstances beyond the control of the parents—like those exploding hormones—affect children.

The answer? Keep your head, ride it out, and don't overreact every time your kids are moody, moderately disrespectful, or want to spend more time with their friends. Stay involved, keep trying to program fun activities together, and definitely be interested in them and uncompromising in your love for them and belief in them.

Communication Killer #4: Not Recognizing That Your Relationship Goes through Stages

"When my son was in about fifth or sixth grade," a friend told me, "I really made an effort to treat him like a fellow human being. On many occasions I'd talk to him, ask questions, and relate to him as if I weren't the dad. I acted like I wanted—and really desired—to have fun with him."

That type of realization is a wondrous thing.

During the later grade school years, you're moving toward the ultimate transition: preparing your son to leave the nest. Right now you're in the parent-disciplinarian-teacher mode. As he gets into his teen years, it turns more into the parent-teacher-counselor mode. By the time he's in late high school and early college, it becomes the parent-counselor-friend mode. What you're leading to is the parent-counselor-friend mode. This is exactly where you want to be, but you have to go through all the stages to get there. Remember when Jesus said, "I no longer call you servants, because a servant does not know his master's business. Instead, I have called you friends, for everything that I learned from my Father I have made known to you" (John 15:15)? Even the disciples' relationship with Jesus "grew up." So must your relationship with your son. And by recognizing the stage you're in—and the next one on the horizon—you're doing your job as a dad to get him ready to leave the nest as a normal human being (who has a good relationship with his parents).

Communication Killer #5: Not Understanding the Changes Kids Go through in the Different Phases of Life

Sadly, many dads figure that once they graduated from school (college or high school), they received a lifetime deferment on learning. But since you have this book in your hands, it's obvious you're trying to expand your knowledge about parenting.

Even though I worked with teenagers for twenty years, I still couldn't afford to make parenting up as I went. The youth culture continues to change too rapidly. I had to stay current with the pressures my boys were facing, and so do you. The greater your knowledge of your son's world, the more you'll understand him.

What can you do? Before your son hits his teen years, read and listen to materials about teens to discover the world they're living in. For instance, a dad would do well to glance through Focus on the Family's *Breakaway* magazine for teen guys. The topics written about—peer pressure, bodily changes, relating to the opposite sex—will open a little window for you into your son's future world. Of course, there also are plenty of other materials worth seeking out (books, tapes, and videos) that are produced by those specializing in teen ministry.

The point is, don't think that just because you were a teenager once with active hormones, you automatically know the teen culture. Read books. Take your church's youth leader to lunch and grill him on what he thinks. You can even talk to other dads who are recent empty nesters. The information you'll ingest with just a few hours' effort will be invaluable.

Communication Killer #6: Parental Insecurities

It's tough to admit, but some dads are more insecure than their kids. Somewhere along the line they never gained the confidence necessary to parent—or stand up to an unruly son. When a dad is unsure of his role, he will either overcompensate and be authoritarian or he will undercompensate and get walked over. Because today's society is so much different from the one in which we grew up, some situations and fears are legitimate. Our kids, however, will rebel if our unrealistic fears cause us to be unreasonable. If at all possible, we need to express confidence and trust in our children, as this man's father did years ago:

> Once when I was set to go to a church youth event at a hotel, my dad sat me down to talk. He said he knew there would be guys and gals in hotel rooms, and he mentioned that a girl and a guy could find themselves in a room alone. He said, "I remember what it was like to be in high school at your age. There's a possibility you'll end up alone with a girl in your room. If it happens, I know you'll do what's right."

I didn't give it a second thought, because I knew it wouldn't happen to me. But that weekend I somehow ended up with a girl in my room! I couldn't believe it. I quickly told her good night and she left. It would have been easy to make the decision the other way, but I didn't want to violate that trust and respect he showed for me.

Secure parents trust their kids. Secure parents raise secure kids. Secure kids can be trusted.

Communication Killer #7: A Know-It-All Parent

"If my dad would have asked my opinion on things," one man said, "we would have been friends earlier. Instead we lived in an atmosphere where if I said anything, I got in trouble. I remember saying, 'Other kids don't have to go to church *every* Sunday night.' Dad said, 'You're not other people's kids.' End of discussion."

Know-it-all dads have to win every argument, often invoking either high decibels or their God-ordained role as head of the family. If their goal is controlling behavior, they will rarely admit defeat.

Question: Is it unscriptural for a dad to back down once in a while? What I've heard men say is that when a dad admits a mistake, it actually draws a son closer to him.

Throughout our lives we all learn to either respect or not respect people we've come to know. My "respect-o-meter" goes off the scale when I see someone who can, with humility, admit his faults. I want to hang around that person because he has shown that he is human—just like me. As dads, we have to fight the self-righteous urge and take time to talk things through when there's conflict.

Communication Killer #8: Differences in Values

Our sons won't always accept our values. Their decision not to adopt the attitudes and behaviors we'd like them to is sometimes caused by the three Ps mentioned earlier (puberty, peer groups, and pop culture). Sometimes it's due to a lack of consistency in our own lives. Children are the first to notice if Dad says one thing and does another, and they're not too keen on following in those footsteps. (Who would be?)

Most often, however, an emerging adolescent is simply testing the values he was taught, to see if he wants them as his own. As much as we'd like our sons to believe something because we said it, that doesn't always happen, especially if there are other voices whispering different things—and there are *many!*

One solution is to put as many positive voices as possible into our sons' lives. That's because Satan's attack against their faith and values is occurring on at least eight fronts:

1. The Magazines They Read

Magazines for boys, though specialized and varied, don't always reinforce your values. However, unless you have a son reading magazines about heavy metal music, skateboarding, or surfing (which are pretty raunchy), most are fairly tame. *Breakaway* has an eye-catching design and features Christian sports personalities, music, and other general-interest topics that can really hold the short attention of boy readers.

2. The Music They Listen To

For many boys, music is like air; they have to breathe it in every waking moment. If they're into the latest rap or other new releases, you can be sure many of the lyrics they lip-synch don't reinforce biblical values.

If your son is into music, encourage him to listen to the great Christian alternatives (in every style imaginable!). An older friend of mine said contemporary Christian music had always been a part of his home. The end result? "We've never had a fight about secular rock music. My kids simply weren't interested in it, because the Christian music they had was so good."

3. The Books They Read

Without much effort you can provide a steady stream of interesting books, many from a Christian perspective. Church libraries and public libraries offer volumes of free entertainment. And if you've got enough in the family budget for a $20 per month "book allowance," it will likely be the best investment you can make in your son's reading skills.

4. The Friends with Whom They Associate

Choosing the right friends is a skill, and hopefully you've been teaching this skill since your son was younger. (I'll have a few thoughts on this later.) Now, since the teenage years are imminent, your son should keep right on rolling into friendships with those who have been taught similar values. Although friend making is a little hit-or-miss, you can do your part by constantly reinforcing what it means to be a good friend.

5. The School They're Attending

Parents are faced with a real dilemma about where to educate their children. For instance, the positives of a Christian school or home schooling are these:

- The peer group can generally be controlled.
- Education can often be accelerated.
- The teachers are Christians.
- The curriculum isn't secularized, as it is in public schools.

Some of the reasons for staying in public schools are these:

- Christian school costs can be prohibitive. Home schooling kids takes a patient and motivated parent.
- Children can learn how to relate to non-Christians, hopefully without being negatively influenced themselves.
- If parents are good models, children have an incredible opportunity to reach out to non-Christians.
- It is unlikely kids will become "inoculated" to Christian teachings.

Some parents send their children to a Christian school and expect the school to teach the parents' values. Parents need to take on this challenge, to build communication and cement their relationship with their kids.

6. The Movies They Watch

Dads *can* control this one, although many abdicate their watchdog role. In addition, your strongest argument is, "Your mother and I don't watch those kinds of movies, and I don't think it's out of line to expect that you don't either."

7. The TV They Watch

See communication killer #2. Discernment, discernment, discernment! Live it. Teach it. Reap the benefits for years to come.

8. The Adults in Their Lives

Whether it's teachers, neighbors, coaches, or relatives, other adults can play a significant role in establishing the values of your son. It's impossible to keep him away from every negative influence (you can't lock him up), so you need to be a student of the adults influencing your son. Asking the right questions about these adults (while avoiding unwarranted character comments), especially when he becomes a teen, teaches discernment, shows respect, and allows the boy to value what you do. Often he won't even realize *why* you're asking those questions.

Communication Killer #9: Poor Relationship Skills

I realize that not every dad has the interpersonal relationship skills of a professional counselor, but that's no excuse for not making an effort. One pastor who has watched dozens of children rebel against their families points to this issue as a major contributing factor. "You can't justify the lack of relational skills as a dad," he says. "No matter what you were taught or how you were raised, you need to work hard at communicating with your son. Too many dads settle for the status quo and don't realize what they're creating in the process."

Whether you tend to be overbearing or someone who can't speak his mind, poor relational skills—especially when your son finally hits the teen years—can be devastating. I used to read letters every week from *Breakaway* guys lamenting how their dads didn't understand them. What they were really saying was this: "They won't spend time listening and talking with me!"

In these days, when so many issues need to be bounced off a caring and involved dad, we simply cannot be unapproachable because we don't have the skills to invite our sons into a heart-to-heart discussion.

Communication Killer #10: Conditional Love

One college student told me,

> When I was fifteen, I started hanging around a group of metal heads. My parents objected and a rift grew in our relationship. But I didn't want to quit spending time with them, and there wasn't much my folks could do.
>
> I quit going to church for a year, even though I still lived at home. Each time the subject would come up, my parents made it clear they couldn't condone what I was doing. But they always told me they loved me. It was very clear to me how they felt—on both subjects.
>
> When I finally found a few new friends, it felt good not to worry about upsetting my parents anymore. They never manipulated me, and that let me see how much I valued their love above a few friends heading in the wrong direction.

Had the parents been relentless to get their way, they would have communicated "conditional love." Because they affirmed the son separate from his behavior, the son eventually *wanted* to make good choices.

Every dad bumps up against some of these communication killers sooner or later. Examine your style of parenting—even your own personality—to see if you have the potential to shut off the flow of quality communication between you and your son. If you do, make the necessary alterations as soon as possible. The teen years come and go too quickly, and you never want to regret what you could have changed.

The truth is, even when we try our best as dads to keep everything great between ourselves and our sons, we'll still make honest mistakes and have to deal with them. In the next chapter John comes back to talk about three primary ways dads tend to confuse their sons, thus harming the goal of building a strong relationship.

5. Turning Wrongs Around (or How to Confuse Your Son in Three Easy Lessons)

Do you remember trying to understand girls in junior high? Figuring out if they *really* liked you or your best friend was next to impossible, even after reading notes captured between classes. But as you know today, the problem of understanding the female species really isn't a junior high problem. It's a *lifetime* problem! The only difference is that today we have a backlog of experience that helps us interpret all the mixed signals. At age twelve of course we didn't have that benefit (not that it would have helped much anyway).

At age eight or ten or twelve, how much experience does your son have at figuring *you* out as a parent? Well, not much, actually. His problems and felt needs are changing so rapidly that you're in a constant state of trying to catch up to the new parenting style he needs from you. The point is that for the prepubescent male, interpreting your signals and your parenting style is a tall order. That's why it's essential to not confuse your son about your thoughts, actions, intent, and style.

But if you want to do it anyway, here are three ways to do it best.

1. Fail to Make Any Tough Decisions (Always Defer to Mom)

My daughter Kari was a precocious twelve-year-old when she came to me one Saturday asking if she could go see a movie with her girlfriends. While I don't remember exactly what movie it was, I remember that it was a movie both Cindy and I thought was questionable for a younger girl. Because all her friends were going, Kari was excited about spending time with them. Instead of being a bit more forthcoming, I deferred to Cindy to let her make the decision. Unfortunately, she wasn't home at the time. (This was before cell phones became a family necessity.) About an hour before Kari was to leave for the movie, Cindy came home. When she found out what movie it was, let's just say we had a "disagreement." Most men are about as sensitive to these types of issues as a shyster used-car salesman is to a fair deal. The united front parents need on close calls wasn't firmly in place, and I was soon shown the error of my ways. Conclusion: "Sorry, Kari, you can't go."

Our bad news to her this day hit too late for her to arrange to do something different with her friends. Her only choice was to stay home. She summed it up in words I've never forgotten: "Dad, that was really crummy parenting!"

Never a truer phrase spoken.

If you want to keep your son confused, keep the rules blurry, defer to your wife on the tough decisions (so she looks like the bad guy), and try not to be on the same parenting page.

2. Overpromising

My own father wasn't around very much, but Greg told me that his alcoholic dad was pretty good at making promises and then not delivering, especially during his darker alcoholic days, before he got sober. It would happen primarily on planned Saturday morning fishing trips. More than a few times Greg would get all the tackle ready the night before, carefully cleaning his gear, getting his pole, creel, and net all laid out so when the horn sounded at 5:00 a.m. (Greg's mom and dad were divorced, so his dad always came early to pick him up), he'd be ready to roll for the two-hour drive up to the reservoir. The problem was, alcoholics are notorious for not following through. So who got to see the heartbreak and try to make last-second plans when the day was ruined? Good ol' Mom.

There was an intern at a church I once served in who was always gung ho about everything. Whenever he was asked to do something, he said he'd do it. About two months into his internship, the staff started to wonder why things weren't getting done. Small tasks that had been delegated to this guy were never completed. Pretty soon the whole staff had a mess on their hands as they tried to clean up this guy's over-promising and underdelivering.

The proverb is true: "Hope deferred makes the heart sick, but a longing fulfilled is a tree of life" (Proverbs 13:12). You don't have to be an alcoholic to be unrealistic with your son. All of us have a tendency to say things to bring a moment's joy, knowing that we may be unable to fulfill the promise we made. To do that with a young son is devastating. It communicates that your word can't be trusted, and as Forrest Gump said, "That's a bad thing."

Say what you plan on doing. Do what you say. You have to be a father whose word can be trusted.

3. Overusing Power Plays

Did you see the movie *October Sky*? The father in the movie is a real hard-guy coal miner. Among other fatherly foibles, he thinks that by yelling at or berating his son, he can somehow stop him from dreaming about his goal to launch rockets.

I don't know if you grew up around anger or bullying, but it may be one of the most destructive forces that can negatively affect a spirited young male. Outbursts of yelling, a constant negative tone of voice, being stared down by this huge male standing over you—all can absolutely ruin the father-son relationship for a lifetime. And when that son becomes sixteen and is taller or stronger than his dad, this is prime territory for the Enemy to do his worst and divide what could and should be a close father-son friendship.

You may think this type of behavior doesn't occur in Christian homes, but I tell you the truth: there are many, many Christian dads who have anger problems. It's beyond the scope of this book to deal with this sad fact in any meaningful way. But if you have an issue with your temper, I can absolutely promise you that unless you deal with it—and soon—there will be lifetime consequences for your son and your relationship with him. Age mellows most men, but by the time they reach their sixties and they've realized what they've done, the long-term consequences have already happened. Your son has grown up with an anger problem and is handing it down to his son as well.

Most men who have an anger problem genuinely love their sons. They just haven't been faced with the long-term consequences of their behavior. These consequences happen slowly and small children are fairly quick to forgive. But if you want to confuse your son for life about your true heart for him, and probably everything you tell him about a loving God, then think your outbursts of anger aren't affecting him. Don't get help. Don't change.

There are probably dozens of other small ways that fathers confuse their sons, but drawing from my own counseling practice and my own family, I can say that these are the main three which tend to do the most damage.

6. Showing Affection

It was the first day of fourth grade for my son Troy, and I had the privilege to drop him off, meet the teacher, and make sure he was all settled. I got out of the car and walked him to his room, where the teacher quickly said he could go out and play with his buddies. After exchanging small talk with her, I went outside to say good-bye.

Troy caught my eye and looked away. *What's going on?* I thought. So I walked over to him on a mission to get that hug and kiss. He looked at me with fear in his eyes. He'd seen the look on my face before. Undaunted and absolutely clueless, I kept walking toward him. And though he stiffened up, he let me give him a hug and a quick kiss on the top of his head.

I discovered later of course that this totally embarrassed him in front of his friends. How did I find out? He told me. Though I was dejected, I realized that my firstborn son had passed a threshold as a young man.

I don't know when it will happen for you, but you must clue in today, Dad. For many boys there is a magic date—and it's different for each kid—when outward signs of affection between you two should be shared privately. It doesn't mean he loves you less; it just means that hugs and kisses will embarrass him instead of being a source of emotional security and affection.

The best way to prevent this from happening is to ask him every year or so what he's comfortable with. A question like, "If I happen to give you a hug when I drop you off or pick you up from school, how would you feel about this?" should give you all the clues you need.

Some kids of course won't mind at all if you hug them in public. They're wired not to care what their friends think. Or they're wired for affection, so don't withhold it from them just because they're getting older.

One big goal as your son grows up is to *never* embarrass him in front of his friends. If you do it more than a couple of times—even accidentally—he'll tend not to even acknowledge your existence when his friends are around. That's the last thing you want. If he feels safe around you when he's with his peer group, however, he'll tend to include you more into his world. If he doesn't feel that safety, he'll look for ways to shut you out. The peer group does take over a bit, but if you respect his boundaries, he'll come back around and be that hugger of a son he once was.

This means you must realize that building your relationship with your son is a constant process that will take some creativity and thought. While you'll always be Dad to him, the transition from grade-school-hero Dad ("Will you buy me a box of baseball cards?") to teenage-years-doofus Dad ("Is the car filled with gas?") is happening. And other transitions lay ahead, when you become I'm-in-college-so-you-now-know-absolutely-nothing Dad ("Can I have forty dollars?") to what I'm told is the payoff period: I'm-married-with-kids-and-you're-smarter-than-I-thought-you-were Dad ("Can I have a few grand for a house?").

But those later transitions are years away, and of course it will be different for you. (Yeah, right.)

Today all you should be thinking about is growing deeper in your relationship so you two are not only still speaking by the time he graduates but have the look of best buds. To do that, you need to work on getting under the surface. Here are a few more ideas.

Go on a "Dream Date"

Every year on or near his birthday, take him out to Denny's and have him write down five dreams he has for his life. This could be a dream for next week, next month, the upcoming year, or his whole life. Just have him write them down so you can save them for him. If he wants to put them in a sealed envelope, no problem. Just keep them in a place where you can access them as he gets older.

By doing this, you'll discover some of his likes. They'll be good to refer back to later when he's seventeen or eighteen and you're discussing what he may want to do in life. A lot of kids at this age, when confronted with *all* there is to do in life, can't decide what to do. By looking back on his dreams, you help him discover what has been in his heart for many years. Though it may not yield anything earth-shattering, it might show a pattern that will turn the light on for him.

By observing my son's now graduated friends, it's obvious to me that boys have a tendency to start heading off the deep end when they have no direction in life. It's not that a young son has to find his life's calling at age seventeen, but there is a security and confidence that happens inside him when he knows what he wants to do. Aimlessness sometimes leads to recklessness, and that's *not* a trait you want him to nurture!

How else can you prevent this tendency to drift? Think way ahead and help him realize just how gifted and talented he really is. You probably won't identify his life's work during his grade school years, but you will be able to see what he naturally gravitates toward. Our oldest son loved athletics. Soccer, basketball, baseball—not a month went by from age seven to seventeen that he wasn't playing a team sport. In high school he played two sports at once (soccer and football) three falls in a row. His ability was matched by his competitive desire. He hated to lose. Though at press time he hasn't settled into a career yet, he's majoring in human performance and exercise science and minoring in nutrition. Why? We made sure he knew that these majors existed. His early life was sports; why shouldn't his future include them as well?

Our youngest son was a bit more of a dreamer. He had some nice abilities in sports, but he wasn't as driven. He read, thought, played, but mainly spent time with his friends. He was and remains *very* social. Again, like our oldest, he hasn't signed any long-term contracts for his life's work, but he's showed where his bents lie. He's good with computers, he's good with math, he's got some penchant for languages, but he's just not interested. He's got to be with people. His future likely lies in ministry or social services.

It's all about being a student of your son. Yes, his future is *his* future, so he needs to do the picking, but you can help the process along by being a rudder while he steers his ship. Keep him pointed in the right direction toward what he truly likes, help him ask himself the right questions, and let God and him determine his destination.

Repetition Is the Main Thing

Think back on your own dad for a minute. If he were with you in the room right now, what could you hear him say? My dad died at age fifty-five, almost twenty years ago, yet I still can hear him speaking phrases he said all the time.

"What are you doing, you hawnyawk?" (I had no idea what this meant, but I think it was a funny way of telling me I was acting like an idiot, without actually using that word. Naturally, I have passed this word on to my sons.)

The rest of his phrases that come to mind aren't suitable for a Christian book. The point is, though I knew he loved me, and he said so often, I can't seem to remember things he said about *me*. Fortunately, I haven't spent my whole life trying to win his approval. God intervened and I started listening to his words of love every day. And these truths of what God thinks have marked me and brought security and peace that nothing else could have.

But I decided early in my fathering that I would consistently say things that my sons could *always* hear. The following phrases, combined with other heartfelt words doled out as needed, are the types of things a boy can never hear his dad say enough:

"Have I told you lately how much I love you?"

"Did you know you're about the greatest son a man could ever ask for?"

"I am so proud of you for . . ."

"God gave you a gift (name one) and I'm so grateful you're using it for him."

"I've seen such growth in your life in the area of _____ that I wanted to let you know I've noticed."

"I appreciated the way you talked to your mother when I could tell she was frustrating you."

"Good night. I love you."

"What can I pray about for you? What's one big thing you'd like God to do?"

"Always remember: God is more crazy about you than I am."

If for any reason I don't live long enough to keep saying these things, I want my sons to hear me anyway . . . loud and clear.

The Truth of Your Words Sets Them Free

My wife and I were sitting with some other parents at a pizza place on a late Saturday night, waiting for our food to arrive. One of my sons was sitting with his friends at a table to my right. I secretly stared at him and had one of those "frozen moments." As he sat there laughing and talking like a real human, I noticed something. He looked . . . mature. My mind did one of those ten-second montages in which suddenly you see your son at every age in his cutest picture.

And now he's nearly a man. A good man. The pride I felt was incredible. I wanted to walk over and give him a huge hug and tell him what I was feeling. Instead I savored that thought for a moment, then went back to my conversation, thinking, *I'll tell him later.*

The next morning I waited for him to wake up, then grabbed him in the kitchen before he poured his cereal. Hugging him, I said in a low voice next to his ear, "I was watching you at the pizza place last night. You looked so much like a man, sitting there with your friends. I just wanted to say how proud I am of you for the person you are and the man you're becoming. You make me very happy, and I'm glad God has allowed me to be your dad."

I felt his smile on my neck.

I did good. It was the right dad-thing to do. I shared my heart, told him the truth; he felt better and I felt better.

I've always been pretty good at catching my boys by surprise and telling them something sappy. In my world, not too many people are taking the time to tell me a heart-to-heart truism about my value in their eyes. Since I know I need it, I like to hand it out to my sons, usually in small doses. Why not too much? Well, I don't want them to get tired of hearing it. The "I love you's" come every day, but with the heart-to-heart stuff that makes them swell up a bit, I tend to be more spontaneous. And I've discovered that different kids need this in varying doses.

Whether your son goes to a public or Christian school, chances are he's not hearing much sappy truth about himself from his classmates. The peer pecking order is taking shape. The insecure ones are unconsciously (and sometimes consciously) doing all they can to put others down to build themselves up. To get caught in the crosshairs of this verbal warfare can be devastating to your son's self-image.

How does a boy react after he's been laid low? Likely he'll either retreat and become invisible or he'll find someone else to step on to prop himself up. Either way, his confidence has been shattered and he's making the wrong choice.

His reaction is not all that untypical.

Do you know the times when *I* start to make wrong choices as a Christian? It's when I haven't paid attention to the truth in a while. Forgetting that I'm a child of the King and that I'm loved beyond my ability to deserve it makes me do and say dumb things. Predictably, believing earthly rules by setting aside the heavenly ones turns me into a different person. As a Christian, this is one reason why being consistently in the Word is so essential. I need to constantly hear words of love and truth so I respond to the eternal kingdom correctly. Reminders are my lifeline between the person God knows I am and the person the Enemy would like to make me become.

Suddenly my occasional sappy words take on a whole new meaning. *My boys need these words to emotionally and spiritually survive, to not lose their way in a world that cannot tell them the truth.*

We sometimes deny that even we old adults need sappy honesty—emotional and otherwise—from our spouse, employer, even our own kids and parents! Yes, we've become accustomed to not receiving it and have adjusted our emotional expectations accordingly, but this doesn't mean we don't love being transported beyond our cold, hard world to the place of . . . truth.

Truth is the key. Jesus said, "You will know the truth, and the truth will set you free" (John 8:32). We need to know it, and our soon-to-be teenagers most definitely need to know it.

Notice that Jesus didn't say "hear the truth." The difference between hearing and knowing sometimes takes a lifetime. Some members of my family have been hearing the truth for decades, but their lives communicate that they haven't come to *know* it. To really know truth, of course, someone must really know Jesus. No other foundation can be built upon. But once this is built—as it hopefully has been for your son—there's a resonance with the truth. God's Spirit supernaturally helps a person discern truth from falsehood. I don't know how God does it, but I've seen it happen. Once you've tasted real truth—and know it—spotting a fake becomes second nature.

Even a second-nature foundation, however, needs the right materials built upon it. And that's where you come in. This construction job may be one of your most important as you participate with God in building your son toward spiritual and emotional maturity. It all hinges on the truth he hears and comes to know in two areas: who he *is* (first and foremost) and what he *does* (careful, Dad, not to become too performance driven).

- Is: "You have come so far in becoming a man this past year. I've noticed how you've matured, and I like what I see."
- Does: "I saw you and Jason talking after Sunday school in the hallway. He was talking and you were listening. I

just noticed how well you seemed to be listening. That's a good trait to have, being a good listener. He's lucky to have a friend like you."

The difference is subtle, but by making both of these types of statements—often—you're participating with God in setting your son free by helping him truly know the truth.

Part Two:
Talking Points

7. The Big Four

Probably no other area needs more discussion, but is less talked about, than sex and females. And while you may think this topic should wait until the teen years—or the week before your son's wedding—you're dead wrong. Our culture is way too sex saturated to think that our innocent little grade school son isn't being exposed to—and perhaps influenced by—the raunch that will only get worse in the world as time goes on.

I've identified what I call the Big Four topics that ought to always be on your mind when looking for golden opportunities for discussion or when thinking of ways to orchestrate teachable moments.

But first let me briefly talk about the reasons why men don't major in this area that every man knows is a major area:

1. guilt about our own adolescent failures
2. guilt about our own adult failures (both past or present)
3. ignorance about what topics to cover at each stage in our son's maturity
4. fear

For the record, let me say that none of these reasons is good enough for us to keep silent. So even if all four of them apply to you, get over yourself and start thinking about that precious son of yours. He needs truth, he needs a fearless dad, he needs a knowledgeable dad . . . and you know this one: he needs a dad whose life is backing up his words and beliefs. (There are books written about this topic of being a consistent Christian dad, so I won't take the space to delve into this all-important topic. Suffice it to say, do everything within your power and God's power to get your own life together—and don't rest until you do.)

What are the Big Four areas to always be aware of and to talk about?

1. changes in his body
2. girl facts
3. sexual issues
4. honoring women

Changes in His Body

If you have an eight-year-old, you probably have a few years to start learning before you start teaching. Whatever you do, don't abdicate this job to the schools. The films your boy will see are fine but they're nothing like what you can do. The whole point of this book is to get your relationship ready to handle the tough issues with your son. Again, without that bank vault full of great memories and mature habits of talking and listening, he'll go elsewhere for his information.

So right now you're building the relationship between you two, and now he's starting to become aware that God has made him male, that he's getting bigger, and that somehow there's this thing called sex. He doesn't have a clue how it all fits together . . . but you do. And lucky you, you get to start talking about all this, fortunately beginning with an area that is pretty nonthreatening: his body. All you have to do is take the initiative and you'll continue to be the dad who knows everything. (Relish this as long as you can.)

This isn't "the talk" yet, so you're off the hook for a while. It's simply keeping him informed about what's ahead. In a low-key way, you talk about muscles getting bigger, voice changing, acne starting to appear, a soon-to-come sudden interest in girls (and his own appearance), pubic hair, and when the time is right in his maturity, nocturnal emissions and the rest.

How do you best get all this information across?

Be a student of his every change, so you have a hot climate for learning.

Question: When will your son be most interested in driving a car? When his feet can reach the pedals? When he's almost fifteen? When his older brother starts driving? Basically, it happens when his ability to drive is nearing reality. You likely won't give him a driver's manual at age nine and tell him, "Get ready, because in six years you're going to need to know this."

The same is true about all these guy-girl-sex issues. If you warn him too far ahead of time, it'll go in one ear and out the other. If you wait too long, you'll be perceived as being out of touch ("Dad, I already know all this"). That's why you must be a student of his every change.

So when do you bring things up? Answer: All the time, in the right way, in his own time, at his own place of maturity.

Puberty isn't an event as much as it is a process, so you have to let him know that you're the expert on *his* process. One note: If he's a late bloomer, don't wait until his maturity starts showing. He's likely got friends who are maturing early, so he's going to need to get the right info from you a little before he's "ready." (This means you're going to have to be a student of all his friends too.) And if he is a late bloomer, let him know how okay this really is, tell stories about yourself, and always reassure him that he's normal for him and it won't be long before all his friends are close to the same level of maturity.

Should you participate in Dr. Dobson's "Preparing for Adolescence" weekend with your son? Absolutely! But this should never be a substitute for ongoing small talks about incremental changes in his maturity. Remember, what you're doing in all this is showing that you're a fearless and knowledgeable dad who can be trusted.

And speaking of trust, you can't afford to ever lose it in this area.

Ever.

That means that you never, *ever* tease him about the changes he's going through. Not in front of others (girls, friends, Mom, grandparents) and not even when you're one on one with him. I can't stress this enough. These years are already such an insecure time for him that if his own dad starts to make fun of him for some cheap laughs, he will *really* retreat into himself for protection. That doesn't mean he won't be getting information, because he will (and usually from the wrong sources). He just won't be getting it from you. That's not what you want, right? So always know that you and your son will deal with man-to-man issues like two men talking about really important things. There's mutual respect that happens when you respect his privacy about his changes and he respects your knowledge and concern.

Girl Facts

The female species will always be a mystery to your son, evidenced by how much they are still a mystery to you. But confidence comes with knowledge, and insecurity comes with ignorance.

I don't know about you, but I wanted my sons to be confident and secure around girls. I'm not sure I succeeded but it wasn't for lack of effort. I was always talking about little things they should know about girls.

- "Every girl is progressing on her own timetable. Don't make fun of the tall girls or the ones who have to wear bras in grade school." This helps him to accept his own timetable as perfectly normal.
- "Never comment on girls' body parts." He would not like it if others commented on his shortcomings, so he must realize that any talk of weight, hair, pimples, breasts, backsides, and hairy legs are always off-limits.
- "Realize that girls mature earlier than guys." This means they are starting their menstrual cycle and are very sensitive about it. This discussion can happen the first time he notices that Mom is moody or cranky. The same rules of behavior toward girls his age apply to Mom. This issue is never to be anything more than a fact of life, something God created for a reason, and is nothing to be made fun of. And yes, you should explain the biology of it all and how important it is because he will want children someday, and you will want grandchildren to spoil.
- "Girls are real people and it's hard to be a girl." Sadly, our culture doesn't place a huge emphasis on the true value of a woman. There is an idealized and unapproachable standard that women feel they must somehow live up to and it causes them to be very insecure— about almost everything. Tell him, "You, as a male, can either feed this insecurity or do things that build up the

girls around you." This was a constant talk I had with my sons. Whether it was after watching particularly degrading commercials or TV shows, I brought this up a lot. One warning: The older boys get, the less this lesson sinks in. If it's not drummed into them early, the peer group's opinion can sometimes win the day.

I'll deal with this in a bit more depth when I talk about honoring women, but for now these are the basic girl facts of which your young son must be made aware.

Sexual Issues

I had "the talk" with both my sons. And while they probably can't remember it, for me it was a turning point in how I viewed them. They were no longer little boys but maturing males about to enter the big, bad world, where they'd be exposed to things I wish could be avoided.

"Son, sex will be one of the most enjoyable experiences you'll ever have, but if or when it's misused, it also has the potential to ruin your life."

With these words I embarked on a monologue (don't expect a lot of questions) of body parts and body fluids and "real men wait until marriage for sex" and other areas equally uncomfortable, odd, but somehow fulfilling to talk about with my son. They were both twelve when the talk occurred.

I talked about how when a man looks at a woman's naked body in person or in pictures, a pleasurable hormone is secreted in his brain. (And later, as they hit their teen years, I talked about how overuse of this "eye pleasure" can warp his view of women and cause addictions he won't want to have later in life.) I also talked about masturbation, and sheesh, was that a difficult discussion. But nothing was out of bounds. Ever.

The opening rounds in these issues must be timed correctly. Bring it up too early and you'll get blank stares (and the information won't stick). Bring it up too late and you'll be viewed as behind the curve, hopelessly lost in the seventies and eighties, before there was sex. Timing is everything.

At this point I'm going to defer the finer details of this topic to three books that I consider must-reads for any dad: *Every Man's Battle*, a book for men that will give you some tools to help you handle your own lingering sexual issues; *Every Young Man's Battle*, a frank book for guys in their teen years; and a book due out in fall 2003 called *Preparing Your Son for Every Man's Battle* (all written by Stephen Arterburn, Fred Stoeker, and Mike Yorkey, published by WaterBrook Press). This topic is simply too big for this book and too important to gloss over.

Ongoing discussions about this huge issue will not only protect your son from a lifetime of heartache (and possible sex addiction) but it will cement your relationship for life.

The most important thing you (and your wife) can possibly do is to *continually* talk to God about this issue on behalf of your son. You'll need every heavenly influence possible working on your son's behalf. Pray, pray, and pray.

Honoring Women

If there is one phrase you need to wear out your son with, it's "honor women." When he looks lustfully at a girl, these two words need to zoom right into the moral void and make him take action in the battlefield of his mind. I don't have to tell you what uncontrolled lustful thoughts and actions can have on your marriage (not to mention your walk with God). Just think if these two little words had been drilled into your head during your formative years. You'd likely not have as much to regret.

Fortunately, you're at the exact right time to begin the process. How do you do it?

First, make honoring your wife one of your life missions. She is worthy of honor as the mother of your children, she is worthy of honor as the one you are challenged to love "as Christ loved the church" (Ephesians 5:25), and she is worthy of honor because she is a unique creation of God for whom Christ died. If this isn't one of the highest missions you have, it won't be one of your son's missions in life, either.

The best part about this mission is that it's never too late to start. Even if you've been an insensitive sort of a husband for fifteen years, you can change the way you look at and act toward your wife . . . today! Your son will best catch what honoring is about by watching you in action.

Do you do the little things she asks, without complaining?

Do you bring her small presents that communicate that you value her?

Do you bless her in front of your son for who she is as a wife, mother, and child of God?

Do you touch her and hug her appropriately, showing her value as a human being?

Do you speak words of love that affirm your commitment to her for your lifetime?

Do you praise her not just for what she does but for who she is?

The answer to all these questions for me of course is no. I'm human and I forget about such important things, especially when I'm hungry, amorous, tired, working on a project around the house, amorous, or when sports are on the tube. But I am the type to do *some* of these things, albeit sporadically, and I know I have the *potential* to do most of them fairly consistently. It's sort of the Romans 7 syndrome. I know the right thing to do but I just can't do it! I have that sin-nature thing going on, but I've also been freed from this struggle by the resurrection of Christ and his victory over my sin.

And that's what I want to challenge you to realize: you can have a resurrection in how you treat your wife. All it takes is repentance of your past mistakes (confession and turning around—to God and your wife), and a renewed commitment to honoring that peach of a gem who puts up with all your male foibles (most of the time) and sticks with you.

So let's review.

First, start over and start honoring her.

Second, say the phrase "honoring women" a lot around your son. Let him grow up weary of hearing about it, because this is exactly what he will then hear when he's tempted to do anything else. (And guess what, he's going to be tempted!)

Third, develop a "ten commandments of mom honor" that both you and your son can commit to memory. But instead of "thou shalt not," make it more positive.

> I *will* look for ways to make my wife's job as a mother easier around the house.
> I *will* never be sarcastic to her to get a cheap laugh from my dad (or son).
> I *will* value her words.

And so on. You need to struggle with your own list. Own it. Use it. Memorize it. Live it. If you follow no other suggestion in this book, follow this one. Your wife will thank you and his future wife will thank you (and if he *does* learn the secret of honoring his woman, *he* will thank you because he'll have a wife who will learn how to honor him).

In summary, these Big Four areas have to be a constant subject of discussion and modeling in order for your son to enter adulthood more normally than you did. It's a sexual jungle out there, with dozens of predators lurking in the shadows. If you're not making this a source of prayer, education, prayer, and discussion, plan on bearing some heartache for your son in this area.

8. Defining Real Christian Manhood

I wrote a book a few years ago for teen guys, called *Man in the Making*. I identified thirty-five topics for guys to pay attention to as they grow from being young teenagers to being older teenagers on their way to adulthood. It challenged young men to improve one step at a time, without the pressure of ever thinking they had to be perfect.

Have you ever defined "real Christian manhood"? Do you know what it looks like? Is it right behavior? Is it saying the right things at the right time? Or is it perhaps being someone who is clean-cut and never causes problems?

If you have not identified this approximate destination for yourself, it will be extremely hard to take your son on this all-important journey. Success in getting to a place you haven't been before (raising your son to Christian manhood) won't happen without a map. This short chapter is going to help you start creating that map so both you and your son can get on the right road. However, it won't be a point-by-point road map in which each destination puts you on the road to the next. There are no easy interstate highways that avoid every side road or pothole along the way.

Parenting a son to real Christian manhood is the art of staying on course, knowing when to hit the accelerator and when to tap on the brakes, understanding that hundreds of smaller detours will be made, that rest areas are an important part of the journey, and that you can personally only travel so far with your son in this quest. There comes a time when he must take the wheel and head off to that destination alone with God. (Hopefully, God will be driving.)

Creating a Hunger for the Journey

Anticipation about the journey to Christian manhood is a lot like the feeling one gets when looking forward to a long-awaited vacation.

If there was one thing I was good at while the boys were growing up, it was investing in vacation memories. We took some great ones. The first big one was a two-week trip through the Midwest to see seven major-league baseball games in five different parks. (Three of the parks are no longer in existence.) We also made stops at Dyerson, Iowa (where the real "Field of Dreams" is located), Chicago, and Lake Erie. Another year we drove through twenty southern states on our way to Orlando and Washington, D.C. We saw the Civil Rights Museum and Graceland in Memphis, Civil War battlefields, all the sights in D.C., even the Louisville Slugger baseball bat factory. Another summer we hit the East Coast, going to Cooperstown, Yankee Stadium, the Basketball Hall of Fame, and Plymouth Rock, taking a boat trip around Manhattan, and spending a day at a New Jersey seashore.

We involved the boys in planning where we'd go, choosing things they wanted to do as well as things we thought they'd like to do. The anticipation about each day was phenomenal, but nearly every day was hard. Miles in a van (even a nice one) weren't always fun. But the reward of experiencing new things each day made the trip worthwhile. It was an everyday adventure that has given my sons lifelong memories.

That's what the journey to Christian manhood must do for your son. You must talk about the rewards of the destination (though you and I know it's really not a firm destination but a continual journey) but not gloss over the conditions of the trip. The end result is that feeling in your son that real Christian manhood is one of the best—yet toughest—goals he can shoot for, and he is self-motivated to take it, with and without you.

Describe and Define the Big Markers

If you made a list of what a Christian man is and isn't, what would that list contain? Mine would have these elements:

- He isn't perfect; he is real about his fallen state and relies on Jesus Christ day by day.
- He isn't performing for God or others; he is attempting to be real and honest about his failures and successes.
- He doesn't dread the journey; he enjoys the journey, knowing that God loves him no matter what he does or doesn't do for God.
- He isn't bitter about the hard things that come his way; he is thankful for each new experience because it prepares him for the future and gives him depth to help others.
- He is perceptive enough to learn from his mistakes and mature enough to not keep making the same ones over and over.
- He isn't impatient with the rest areas and pit stops along the journey; he welcomes the chance to slow down and look back on where he has been, so he can make the miles ahead even better.

Do you get where this is going? Defining the broad strokes of where you're headed—both for yourself and your son—will give you "markers" along the way to help you determine whether you're going in the right direction. These markers are more like foundational-knowledge principles necessary to make the journey joyful than like specific road signs that define the rules of the road. You don't need too many of them, five to ten at the most.

Rules of the Road

Traffic lights and road signs, combined with a good knowledge of the rules of the road, keep millions of drivers relatively safe each day on thousands of roads and highways throughout the country. We (generally) obey the speed limit, follow the signs, and keep in step with common courtesies. The result is that a very high percentage of people reach their destination in one piece. And when they don't arrive safely, it's often because some rule was violated or they succumbed to distractions.

Christian manhood has some rules of the road that need to become second nature to your son. Here is a short list of some of the things I've always taught my sons to follow so they get to this all-important destination:

- Never act as if you're perfect or better than others.
- Love God and others.
- Kindness and niceness will always get you further in life than insisting on your own way.
- Don't ever shut out from your life anyone who would willingly die for you (God, your family, close friends). Though it's true that only God will always be right in the advice he gives, counsel from these others should always be considered before major decisions are made.

- Appearance does *not* make the man. Look as good as you can, but be comfortable and at home with who you are, including all the physical "imperfections" you think you have.
- Serve people, use things—not the other way around.
- An attitude of gratitude will bring you more happiness than any other internal quality you could possess.
- Like few other things, work gives you the sense of accomplishment you need to live a fulfilling life.
- Do everything you do as if you were doing it for the Lord (Ephesians 6:7). Always seek to play to an audience of one.
- Laugh a lot and help others do the same. Life is too short to take it or yourself too seriously.
- The greatest use of life is to live it for something that will outlast it.
- "As far as it depends on you, live at peace with everyone" (Romans 12:18).
- Saying the words "I'm sorry" (and really meaning them) is what real men do when they intentionally or unintentionally hurt others.

The idea isn't to make an exhaustive list that becomes too overwhelming for your son to follow, but rather to create a "code of life" that becomes second nature in all his dealings with God, others, and himself. If I had it to do over again, I would buy a small journal of some sort and work on this code together with my boys. Writing things down always solidifies the truths you discover.

The Vehicle

It's impossible to get to your destination without the right vehicle to take you there.

The vehicle to get your son to real Christian manhood, of course, must be driven by the Lord and not by your son. Let me illustrate.

Around town and on your family vacations, you and your wife are the drivers. Your kids, sitting in the back, don't give their safety a second thought. They can play and sleep and gaze out the window without ever wondering if you will get them safely to your destination. There is a trust based on experience. It's that same type of childlike trust that we are encouraged to have in God as he's driving us on our own journey through life.

When my oldest was learning to drive, I was pretty much a tense bundle of nerves. Sitting in the passenger seat while he had control of the wheel left me far from the peaceful trust he had while I drove. But what happened over time was that he built up a good track record for safety, and I began to relax. He was eighteen when he drove to Denver from our home in Colorado Springs (about sixty miles), and I adjusted the seat back and took a short nap. He had arrived as a driver. I could rest knowing that his skills and experience would get us safely to our destination. I trusted him.

It's hard for boys to have that childlike trust in someone they can't see. For some reason, most girls are able to grasp "letting go and letting God" better than boys. And while he may have borrowed your faith and trust in a good God, that will soon be tested. He needs a lesson of what real faith in action truly is about. This illustration of God driving and me learning to trust him at the wheel has served me well in teaching real faith to my boys.

God wants to be the driver on your son's journey, but it will take time for your son to learn to trust God's knowledge and experience. Pride often keeps boys (and men) from trading places with God and allowing him total control of the vehicle (their life). What you are able to do during these years between eight and twelve is to show that God can be trusted with something as big as a life.

"We're down to one thousand dollars in our bank account, Son. I can't wait to see how God is going to provide for us."

"Grandpa has a bad sickness, but he gave his life to Jesus Christ years ago and he's comfortable knowing that whatever happens, he'll be taken care of just fine."

"Mom lost her job, so we're going to have to cut back some on our spending. Looks like this will be a good test of how much we trust in God's provision."

Speaking words of faith and trust instead of doubt and fear will show your son that God is a God who can be trusted in literally *everything*. And faith that God can be trusted to be the driver of his life will insure that he has a fighting chance at developing into the real Christian man you hope he becomes. Without faith—without letting Jesus take the wheel—it is impossible to please God (Hebrews 11:6).

One good way to do this is to find many of your own illustrations and teachable moments for your son to learn from, so it's obvious to him that faith is how the Christian life is really enjoyed.

Following are a couple of practical ways to help convince him that real Christian manhood is a goal worthy to reach for.

Manhood Ceremony

A good friend of mine has Scottish roots. He picked up a tradition that almost makes me wish I were Scottish myself. When the son hits a certain age, the dad invites some key men and their sons to witness a "manhood ceremony."

It's the point at which the dad feels the son has matured to the level where he is ready to consider himself a man. My friend called us all together to witness this ceremony. He read some heartfelt words he had written about the son's maturity, a few other men talked about the boy's manhood, prayers were said, and a traditional Scottish kilt was given to him.

This type of rite of passage is a key time for the son, as he now starts thinking himself a man and not a boy (a significant turn in the mind of a male, one that doesn't happen for some guys until they're suddenly a father—or later still).

Besides the kilt, I wish I would have done this for my own sons. A ceremony in which a dad and others share their heart about a boy's maturity, I think, would bond the dad and son together for life. In this particular ceremony there were tears and hugs and long looks of love between dad and son that would be hard to duplicate outside of such an event.

Though your son is still young, it's not too early to get this on your agenda for down the road.

Yearly Letters

Your son is at the perfect age for you to start writing him handwritten annual letters about real Christian manhood. He may hear your words on this topic, but he will read and reread the letters you've written to him about his ever grow-ing maturity. You start out telling him the facts you never want him to forget: that you love being his dad and you'll love him forever no matter what. Then you go into how you've seen him grow as a man during the past year. You end with more words of affection and with what is your hope and prayer for the coming year. You can even write out your prayer for him. Next create a special "man box" (it could be as simple as a slightly decorated shoe box) in which to store the letters, and he's got something he'll keep his entire life (and something he'll do with his son).

Part Three:
Entering His World

9. Making the Most of School: Setting Him Up for Future Success

Whether or not you were a good student, whether or not you were a success in your work without a college degree, he must sense a high value for education. Where does this value start? How does it continue?

1. A love for learning
2. A knowledge of good study habits

With your wife, this is one area that is most definitely a team effort. If your wife is the lifelong learner and you're the hard worker who is bushed at the end of the day, there is a good chance your son may lose whatever desire to learn he gained in the grade school years. The reason is that a boy wants to be like his dad. And if dad is getting by without expanding his mind spiritually and in the world, he eventually will too. Is that what you want? Do you want him to "get by" as perhaps you have?

How do you build a love for learning?

*   Keep books out on end tables and get caught reading them. I'm constantly reading history books about the Civil War and the American Revolution eras. Whenever I learn something fascinating from those time periods, I'll share it.

- Enjoy museums together. My son Drew and I had the chance to go to Europe several years ago, and we went to the Louvre in Paris, the British War Museum, and a couple of other museums. He loved it, but the reason is that we went to local museums when he was younger.
- Find your son's area of educational love and do things that will cause him to grow in it. I have a friend whose son is into geography. He picked it up at an early age, and through the encouragement of dad (and mom), at age thirteen he won the state geography bee (and a huge scholarship to a private college) and placed high in the nationals.
- There are dozens of magazines for kids on a lot of special areas of interest. If he likes geography, fishing, astronomy, sports, or science, there is a magazine just for him.
- Don't quit reading to them just because they hit age ten. Change what you read, the time you read, the location . . . but keep up the pace until you see him reading by himself out of his own love for it.
- Don't forget about tutors. If he's weak in a core area, start young enough to help him catch up. Troy was taught "whole language" in California for his first two years of grade school, and by the time we moved to Colorado, he was two years behind in reading. We didn't get a tutor, and really regret it. He's in college now and is only now getting a love for reading.

Reading!

Troy was ADHD (Attention Deficit Hyperactivity Disorder) and we didn't find this out until the fall of his senior year of high school. He always had a hard time liking to read, but he did his busy work so well that we didn't notice he was behind the curve a bit. I read stories to both of my boys from age two to ten. We had books all over the house yet Troy still struggled.

That's why for the sake of your son's Bible reading and college future you need to do everything you can to help him love reading. Buy *Hooked on Phonics* if you have to, but don't let him (if you can help it) be like so many guys who are four grades behind in their reading skills.

As your child gets older in his grade school years, the best thing to do is to have him read to you, rather than you always reading to him. This will give you a clue as to where he is in his reading level. And Dad, if you're not exactly a great reader yourself, this isn't an excuse you can use to not do all you can to put your son over the top.

The key with any skill is to teach a love of it. If you're reading books, he'll read books. If you're always watching TV, guess what? He'll always be watching TV. You need to have books he would enjoy to read always close at hand. Should you reward him for reading books (as in five dollars a book)? If you can afford it, absolutely! Guys are motivated by rewards, and if he's struggling, it may be just the thing to give him a little push. Make some trips to the local library and find books that catch his interest. The same is true of magazines. Find a couple he *will* read, and subscribe to them. The key is to not let him fall behind. His educational future may hinge on how good a reader he is. The SAT and ACT tests—which often directly determine what type of college he can get into—reward students who can read quickly with understanding. In this age of information, those who can process a lot of information quickly will succeed in their professions.

If you have a son who's not "bent" in this direction, you may be stuck. There's nothing wrong with being a blue-collar worker or in a profession in which a high level of reading skill is not essential. But the job market each year for college graduates is definitely more competitive than it used to be. Get your son ready now by doing all you can to teach a love for reading. It will be one fatherly emphasis you will never regret.

10. Sports and Competition: What to Expect from Different Types of Sons

Athletics are huge for boys. If you weren't an athlete, if you hated athletics, or if you still can't shoot a basket unless it's a Nerf hoop attached to your son's closet door, that doesn't mean your son won't be—or won't want to be—an athlete. Yes, athletics can make a kid have an artificially inflated view of themselves, it *can* cause them to sometimes act like jerks on the playing field (embarrassing you to no end), and it may force you into getting off the couch to help them learn some things, but it's also a fact of life in our culture.

I had one over-the-top athlete and one normal athlete. And we could have predicted at about age five exactly what their future in sports would be. Boys are just not that hard to figure out. He'll either be aggressive and competitive or more passive and interested in other things. Yes, there is some middle ground, though young boys have a tendency to be microcosms of what they'll become.

Troy was "do or die" in everything he participated in. He performed well in all sports, he sometimes made us look like bad parents by being a poor sport (though not nearly as often as he made us feel proud for his wholehearted effort), and he wasn't a great performer in school. Did we threaten him if he didn't behave or get better grades? Nope. Troy was Troy. He was always his true self when he was competing. Along the way he learned about sportsmanship (eventually), and he learned the hard lessons that it takes work to excel at something, that practice makes almost perfect, that there are coaches who know more than he does, and that it's not all about him. Pretty good lessons, I'd say, that will serve him his entire life.

The thing is, we let him be himself instead of molding him into a boy he wasn't meant to be.

Drew had about half the drive that Troy got and about half the natural ability. He wanted to have fun playing sports, win when he could, but mainly just be with his friends. He had a much more developed creative side, was better in school, and had broader interests. He was a "noticer." He learned by observing and asking questions. Would it have been fun to have two top athletes in the family? Yep, but God gifted him in so many other areas than athletics.

You'll know early on where your son's bents lie. Be a student of your son and simply go with what God gave him. Don't try to force him into a mold he wasn't meant to be in. And along the way rejoice often that God has made him as he is. Let him know too where God has gifted him, so he gets a realistic view of his future.

Coaching and Cheerleading

These two things have the potential to either solidify your relationship for life or cause huge rifts that can take years (or decades) to overcome.

My dad coached me a number of times in grade school, so when my boys hit the right age, I coached them if needed. It turned out I was a Little League head coach for ten years, five with each son. I coached basketball from the time Troy was eight until he was about thirteen (in YMCA and club). But there was a time to be done being "Coach Dad." Junior and high school ball helped. I forced myself to make the transition from coach to cheerleader. And as much as I missed coaching, for my sons it was the right thing. They were ready to learn from other coaches. Some dads of course can have this dual role as a dad and coach, but when you double that up in an area that is supposed to be fun, you'll end up with a lot of silence around the house. That's when I made the intentional transition to being a sidelines pop.

Being an assistant coach in the sport of your son's choice is really the best of both worlds. You can hang around your son and his buddies, help them with the finer points of the skills behind the sport, but not carry any of the disciplinarian or bad-guy role that head coaches have to bear.

Cheerleaders are just that: people who lead the cheer. There is an art to it, and if you don't learn to do it right, it will put that dreaded wedge between you and your son.

I was at a soccer match one Saturday morning, doing what I always did, politely yelling at the refs for being blind and not giving our team the advantage they deserved (in an impartial, objective way, of course). I was never abusive and never swore, but I had a way of making my point by helping to make them look less than knowledgeable. In case you don't know, soccer parents are the worst sports in the history of athletics. They can be downright mean. Well, on this particular day the ref was taking it from both sides, and when somehow through the crowd he heard me say something sarcastic, he'd had enough. "You, you're out of here. Leave." I actually walked away without saying a word (because he wouldn't start the game until I was three hundred feet away). I wondered what I'd said that was so bad. I'd certainly said worse.

That was when it hit me: *I wonder how embarrassed Troy is.*

Suddenly it wasn't about me, it was about him (as it should be). I vowed to keep my mouth more closed in the future. And in soccer I was able to do this pretty consistently (basketball was another story—but no ejections).

A dad can ruin his son's play, and his short-term relationship with him, by being too vocal from the stands. No, the son won't always say so, but what kids really long for from their dads are these:

- Verbal encouragement (that isn't too loud or hokey) when they do something good.
- Silence when they do something bad. They know when they mess up, and just because you're embarrassed by what they did on the court or field doesn't mean you have to do something to deflect the shame from you. It's not about you, it's about your son!
- "Coach" from the sidelines very judiciously. Again, unless your son needs some fine point of instruction that only you notice, leave the coaching to the coach. Good ones know how to motivate their players to learn more, so coaches should be allowed to do it at the right time and in the right way.
- As your son gets older, you need to always ask permission to make a comment about his performance. Don't make it a habit to debrief his performance detail by detail after every game. That will make him dread any after-game discussion, because he's going to get knocked down. If you have something constructive to say and he's given you permission to speak, keep your comments to one or two things. Boys can't handle a dozen improvement "hints" all at the same time.

- Fight the urge to coach the coach. Unless a coach is abusive to the kids (in which case he should *always* be confronted), he's doing the best he can. And it's not his job to get your son ready for superstardom. If your son has the potential and the drive, your job in the off-hours is to show him ways to develop his skills. Great athletes aren't made or broken by playing time (especially in grade school). Your son has potential to become a top athlete according to the hours he puts in away from practice and games. If he's *that* good, he'll see the minutes.

11. Free Time and Entertainment

When I was about ten or so, my grandfather opened up for me a world I didn't know existed. He literally showed me the world through stamp collecting. He started small, buying me a United States stamp album. He gave me some stamps to get started, showed me the basics about how to handle and mount the stamps, then sat back to watch where it took me.

I was hooked.

It wasn't long before I wanted to know what other countries' stamps looked like. He gave me a shoe box full of stamps from Hong Kong, China, Japan, Germany, Australia, and Canada. It wasn't long before I got the Senior Statesman Stamp Book and began spending hours organizing stamps from every country in the world. I went to stamp stores and bought stamps through the mail. When my grandpa died, I was given his entire (and very unorganized) collection. Where did he get it from? His grandfather! Suddenly I was the owner of a stamp collection that had some value. It fit my Beaver personality perfectly. I could stay in my room for hours, separating stamps from all over the world, without getting bored. I think my mom worried about me a little, but I was as happy as a clam.

By collecting stamps fairly aggressively for the next ten years, I acquired a love for geography and history that is still with me today.

My grandfather did the same with coins. Starting with pennies, he got me and my brother into looking for and finding "wheatback" Lincoln head pennies, silver dimes, buffalo nickels, and everything else we could get our hands on. Again, hours of fun . . . without the TV droning on and on.

My mom and dad's gig was puzzles. They loved them and gave my brother, sister, and me a love for them too. And we usually put them together in a room that didn't have a TV. We'd listen to music instead, playing one of the records we liked, and then one they liked. (I still listen to Frank Sinatra and Sammy Davis Jr. with fond memories.)

My grandma taught us kids how to play pinochle. Once we were old enough, she'd take her only three grandkids and we'd play four-handed pinochle by the hours. She'd tell stories about World War II and about my mom, and I think we were all in a little bit of heaven together. Careers, Monopoly, Life, and Yahtzee were among the dozens of games we learned and played together as well. (The last time I walked through the game section at Wal-Mart, all those same games were sitting right there on the shelf, plus dozens of others.)

But when my parents were divorced, Dad wasn't around as much, Mom was working and always exhausted, my grandparents got old or died, and guess what was there to fill the void? TV. Yes, it had always been in the home, but it had never really dominated my life.

There's a Reason Why They Call It the "Boob Tube"

I will set before my eyes no vile thing.

Psalm 101:3

If only we would have known and understood this verse from our younger days, I think a lot of the pain caused by bad habits could have been avoided. But for most of us raised in the sixties and seventies, TV was our entertainment and our baby-sitter. And while it wasn't always "vile" during those years, another version of the Bible uses the word *worthless*. Well, yep, that's about what it was. Think *Gilligan's Island* and you'll know exactly what I mean. But because we didn't become ultra-perverts by watching too much TV, we tend to think that it's still fairly harmless.

Buzzzzzzzz. Wrong answer. Thanks for playing.

And the parting gift we've been left with is a lack of sensitivity to what TV can do to our time, our creativity, our future entertainment choices . . . and worst, what we allow our children to watch on the tube.

If I had it all to do over again, I wouldn't bury my TV set in the backyard, as a friend of mine did twenty years ago, but I would be a bit more ruthless on myself and my family about our viewing habits. My dilemma while my kids were growing up was that I was lazy and liked to watch too much TV. Not mindless and sexually suggestive sitcoms, mind you. But our living room was dominated by sports, the History Channel, more sports, war movies, and even more sports.

Not bad stuff.

Just not good stuff. And too much "not good" stuff.

Enough of the true confessions and enough TV bashing. You're the one in control of the remote in your home (well, most of the time), so you have to be the one who decides what is too much for you and your family. All I can say is, TV shouldn't be the dominant form of entertainment or baby-sitting in your home. How do you change that if it's already a family habit?

- *Call a family meeting.* If you're really tired of the boob tube taking up too much of your family's waking hours, call a meeting to set some limits on how much it can be on. Don't make a unilateral decision. Get the whole family on board with the right plan.
- *Set the limits.* Maybe the TV can be on for six hours a day on weekends and two to three hours a day on weekdays, with one or two nights a week and one weekend a month when it's not on at all. Whatever the plan is, it has to be something realistic and attainable. Try out your plan for a month or two, then reevaluate and make adjustments.
- *Fill the time.* This will take some work on your part. Boys are typically doers and not readers (though it may be easier if they are readers). This book has tons of ideas to get you started. And if these ideas aren't enough and you have a daughter or two with your boy, go out and pick up the other books in this series: *Mom's Everything Book for Daughters, Mom's Everything Book for Sons* (both by Becky Freeman), and *Dad's Everything Book for Daughters* (by John Trent). You'll get more creative ideas on how to spend time together than you ever thought existed.
- *Enhance creativity.* Fun and games are great. We all need more of it. Reading is a lost art and should always be encouraged. Computers definitely are the wave of the future, and our boys should be adept at operating them. But the biggest long-term negative result of the TV, video games, VCRs, and DVD players, and so forth is that they do little or nothing to expand our natural bent to be creative. And while some boys would rather play pool or board games or wrestle in the basement or ride

bikes or throw, kick, hit, or shoot a ball of some sort, some boys have an inborn creativity that needs to be fed—by you, Dad. Why you? Because boys want to be like their fathers. And if Dad thinks learning to play a musical instrument or sing, making works of art with his hands, or conducting chemistry experiments in the garage is uncool or unmanly, his son will too.

These years between eight and twelve are likely the last ones you'll get in which to help alter or set some better life-time habits for your son in making choices about viewing, entertainment, and creativity. We're all creatures of habit, so now is the time to guide yourself and your family into rou-tinely spending free time in ways other than watching TV.

Part Four:
Unforgettable Fun

12. Creating Moments He'll Never Forget

Most dads I know understand the value of creating unforgettable memories, but sadly, many don't. They think that life has enough memories, so they don't have to work too hard at creating any.

Wrong!

Unless you plan for memories—especially good ones—not much becomes memorable. The reason good memories are so important is that your son must associate you with good feelings—as many as possible. Why? Because for many dads and sons, hard times come. And without a bank account of good feelings to draw from, it's easier to not work on the relationship. And your relationship with your son will often determine whether he will come to the Lord, come back to the Lord, or stay with the Lord. If he can write you off, he can write God off. Happens all the time. It's absolutely true for some boys: what they feel about you will be what they feel about God.

Scary, huh?

So build those unforgettable memories several times a year. Take lots of pictures and video footage . . . then talk about them often to get him smiling.

As my boys have grown, I've intentionally reminisced with them about what we've done together. The world is a fierce competitor for the affections of your son, so you have to use every bullet in your holster if you're going to fight back.

Mountain Moments

Troy and I were heading up to the Rocky Mountains to fish for the wild and elusive river trout. A buddy of mine had told me where to find some, so we packed up the van (a conversion van that we could sleep in) and beat the traffic up the pass to a campground. It just so happened that on this Friday night, O. J. Simpson was being tracked by police in his white Bronco going down an L.A. freeway. We listened to it all the way up the mountain and through our dinner of hot dogs and chips. Neither of us could believe that O. J. was on his way to jail, or worse.

One memory in the can, we hit the cushions after counting a few stars. The next day we found a couple of nice streams, but Troy was the only one to get a bite. In a little riffle he hooked something and then panicked, falling into the stream up to his thigh. We both let out a little scream and caught each other's eye. He dropped his pole in the water as I leaped across the stream to pull him out. When I retrieved his pole, he had a fish on the line! A fish as big as . . . my pointy finger! Really. No bigger than my finger. We laughed until we cried.

No keepers in the creel, but two great memories that still make him smile. How do I know? He got home from his first year in college and showed me some of the papers he had written. One brought tears to my eyes. I'll pick it up halfway through.

My dad is on the other side of creek, but we are still close enough to stay in contact with each other.

I feel alone, but free in my own right. My dad trusting me at such a young age to have my own direction in doing something by myself.

I need to break this tree limb to sit on the rock where I can cast my line further downstream. So I attempt to do so. I break the limb, but fall straight down into the creek. The water is hitting me like a thousand knives into my body. I am barely able to hold myself up when suddenly strong hands pull me out, as if my life depended on it, which in realizing that I was only a little boy, it probably did. My dad had pulled me out while I was in my apparent state of shock. He asks, "Are you all right, Son?" Trying to be strong-willed, I reply, "Yes." He takes my hand and pole at the same time. And there, on my pole, is a tiny fish that I had caught.

This memory—still vivid in Troy's mind almost ten years later—existed because we climbed in the van and headed up the mountain.

"Dangerous" Moments

I'm not a very big risk-taker. I didn't hunt with my dad while I was growing up (though we did a lot of fishing), and I think my mom was too scared to let him do something even semi-dangerous with me or my brother.

One summer we were on a picnic up in the Oregon mountains with some other families. Someone had brought a two-man life raft to our lakeside eatery, and the dads were taking turns with their kids on little in-and-out trips. Toward the end of the day I was itching for my turn. The wind had picked up a little, and just before we were to head out for fifteen minutes of adventure, my mom tried to discourage the trip. "Greg's never been out in a boat before," she said to my dad, "and you look tired. Why don't you do something else?"

Well, that small challenge was all my dad needed. "Oh, we'll be fine. Greg's been looking forward to it all day." So I strapped on my life jacket, got in, and Dad shoved us off. We were about twenty feet from shore when Dad asked if I wanted to go clear across the lake. Did I? I jumped at the chance to go farther than all the other kids—with my dad. "Let's go," I eagerly said.

Sometimes a husband needs to listen to his wife's intuition.

The wind began picking up even more, blowing us fairly quickly to the middle of this cold mountain lake. On the way back Dad was working up a sweat trying to make the two small oars propel us anywhere against the waves battering our little boat.

Then it sprang a small leak!

I could see a small look of concern cross his face as he began to row furiously back to home base. By the time we finally made it to shore, the little rubber raft was barely floating and dad was near exhaustion. I don't remember the looks my mom and dad exchanged, but I can guess it wasn't too pleasant for my dad.

Dad should have taken me out as he'd promised, wind or no wind. But he let his pride get the best of him. He needlessly endangered us both (mainly him, I think) when he took us out too far.

Fact one: Moms are always protective.

Fact two: Sometimes their protectiveness is unjustified— but sometimes it is very justified.

A few decades later when I had the opportunity to go up into the mountains on a fishing trip with then ten-year-old Drew and another dad and son, I wanted Drew to do something he would never forget: fire a pistol. As a young boy, like most boys, he had a fascination with toy guns and the like, and I knew he'd love it. We were all by ourselves, and my buddy Dave pulled out his .22 pistol, set up a target, and took a few shots. Then I took a few shots. By this time Drew could hardly contain himself. We let him shoot it twice.

Mom wouldn't have approved, but I kept it "safe" and trusted my instincts (and Dave's expertise). The result: Drew had a story and we had a memory.

Everyday Moments

I am the chocolate chip pancake king. Whenever the boys had friends spend the night, one thing they could always count on when we finally woke them up midmorning was Dad making his specialty. I'd alternate with French toast and we eventually bought a waffle maker, but it's the pancakes the boys will make when *their* boys have sleepovers. Guaranteed.

The point is to have many, many traditions and "rules of the road" in your home that he will take with him.

- How you say grace and pray for others.
- Keeping your humor appropriate.
- Never skipping the worship service to play golf or pursue some other hobby.
- Family devotions, however sporadically, will be something you'll want him to do with his family. He has to see it from you to give this a shot himself.

Bedtime Moments

I remember the days at Chuck E. Cheese's when I thought being the human quarter machine would never end. Today I long for those days. Why? Because now I'm the human cash machine. It's not quarters anymore; it's twenties!

I remember the *Odyssey* tapes, the read-alongs, Candyland, and Sunday school drawings. Now it's CDs of music "talent" I've never heard of, car keys that always disappear, and jeans that cost more than my last month's paycheck at McDonald's when I was in high school.

I remember when I'd make sure my sons brushed their teeth, give them both a hug and kiss, and see them jump playfully into bed to gleefully await stories ("Just one more?").

As time has gone by of course things have changed. Some nights around our house, at least one of my boys will head off to bed without even saying good night. They're as tired as I am, they know the drill, and they seemingly have nothing to talk about.

Or do they?

There's a vulnerability to bedtime that I'm not sure ever goes away. No, not every night, to be sure, but even if it's one night in twenty, I think it's worth the effort to check in. Most nights these days I'll stroll in after they've crawled into bed and ask one or two questions. Their response is the gauge I use to determine whether I stay to chat or simply say, "I love you, Son. Sleep good."

"How'd the day go today?"

"What was the best thing that happened to you today? The worst?"

"What's new with . . . ?" (Insert the name of a friend or the new female attraction.)

"Anything we need to talk about?"

"Want to hear what happened to me today?" (This one doesn't work too often.)

"Anything going on I need to know about?"

"Are you looking forward to anything?"

"Anything fun you want to do together this weekend?"

Most nights nothing happens. But one night not long ago my oldest was despondent over girl problems. He'd just spent an emotional hour on the phone with his girlfriend, and it looked like curtains for the relationship. "Dad, would you pray for me?" He didn't want advice (as much as I wanted to give it) or even a listening ear. I sat next to him, laid my hand on his shoulder, and prayed for him for about a minute. And while I pray for him often, it had been over a year since he'd asked for it. Tell me what I'd trade for that minute!

If it hasn't already, the bedtime routine will no doubt change at your home too. But don't let it disappear completely. The teenage years go by too fast to abandon them to fatigue and changing sleeping patterns. Your son still needs to see your concern, even if he rarely acknowledges it.

Holiday Moments

When my sons were in their early grade school years, I started buying porcelain houses. I'd arrange them all into a "city" that included cars, trees, people, ice-skating ponds, even a railroad that circled the town. And when it was all lit up, well, it was pretty cool. I started with three houses. Ten years later I have over sixty! Each year on the day after Thanksgiving we break out the big boxes, set up the plywood base, and try to recreate last year's masterpiece. When my boys start their own families, I intend to give them their favorite houses so they can start their own cities. (And I'll finally be able to buy the more expensive houses in the specialty shops, rather than the K-Mart cheapies I've accumulated over the years.)

Also at Christmas my wife and I buy each son his own handpicked (semi-expensive) ornament. Again, the intent is that when they leave home, they'll have a boxful of memories to take with them.

Whether it's your Christmas Eve or Christmas Day traditions of watching moves (*It's a Wonderful Life* and *The Gathering* are two of my favorites), viewing the Passion scene in the old *Jesus of Nazareth* movie at Easter, or not eating turkey on Thanksgiving until halftime of the second NFL game, holiday traditions need to be a priority. When your son gets older and is out on his own, you want him to have fond and warm memories of what his family did to make them special. And while one good goal is to pass down traditions that his new family will enjoy, another important goal is to make him long for the predictability of home in case he ever becomes a short- or long-term prodigal. More than one son has returned to the fold because his holiday memories—and the realness of their warmth—drew him back to his roots.

13. Creating Things He'll Never Forget

Moments that yield lifetime memories are the building blocks for a strong relationship you'll always share with your son. And while there is no substitute for these memories, you can't stop there. I have some good recollections of Dad and me, but I possess nothing that exhibits his handiwork. After I became a dad, I realized that I wished I had something that bore his thumbprint, figuratively speaking. So I decided that when I could, I would write or make things that my sons could look at decades later (perhaps when I'm gone) and think, *My father's own hands created this for me.*

Messages in a Bottle

My oldest son doesn't remember it, but when he was eleven, we built a small bookcase to put his stereo and junk on. I'm absolutely a doofus when it comes to woodworking, but we did some measuring, drew up some plans, bought the wood, pulled out the tools, and got busy. The three-by-four-foot bookcase sat next to his bed for six years. He recently moved into his own place, likely never to return home except for visits. He took everything that's his, including our little woodworking project.

Unbeknownst to him, on the bottom of that bookcase I had written a little message six years earlier. Something like, "Troy: You and I built this together on August 11, 1996. And I just wanted to write a little note that will remind you that I'll always love you more than my life. I'll always be your biggest fan. Never forget that. Love, Dad."

At the time of course I didn't know when he'd discover this little "message in a bottle," but I knew that one day he would.

It was moving day in the late summer of 2002 and he had loaded the bookcase into his car for the one-hour drive to Denver. He hadn't noticed anything as he wedged it into his Subaru Outback. When we arrived at his place, we began unloading his stuff. Still nothing. Then his roommate noticed some writing on the bottom of the bookcase as he carried it into the house. "What's this?" he said.

Troy came over. "What's what?"

"This writing." He began to read it out loud. I stopped in the hallway and looked at Troy while he read it silently to himself.

The roommate filled the silence. "Uh-oh. Father-son hug moment."

Troy smiled sheepishly as I walked over to hug him. You don't have to guess what emotion tugged at my heart.

His hug and that look was worth the wait.

The Journal

Probably the best thing I ever did for my sons was to start a journal before they were born. A close friend told me that he was keeping one, and it sounded like a good idea. So I started to write letters to my unborn first son. Nothing long or flowery, just some deeply felt prose that he could look back on one day to allow him to catch a glimpse of my heart. When my second son came along, I included both of their names because my feelings for both were obviously the same.

I've been keeping that journal for twenty years. And while my entries as my sons got into their teenage years were far less frequent than when they were grade-schoolers, they will not be able to miss the message: Dad is crazy about his sons. Along with lots of words of affection are all the lessons I learned from God through my boys while I was learning how to parent. It's a rich treasury that will be the first thing I grab should the house ever catch fire. Through their teenage years I have read certain passages to them when I've felt the need to repair something between us. And while it elicits some rolled eyes and groans when I do, they have no doubts about Dad's love and commitment to them.

(Guess what will be the first thing I'll buy for them when they announce to me they're going to be fathers?)

The Almanac

I have another friend who has put together a 365-day "almanac" of his family, beginning when his first of three sons was born. He wasn't a long-journal-writer type, but he could put in a sentence for big days. He has every major and minor milestone recorded in this almanac. Everything from first teeth, first steps, first T-ball hit, to first date. My boys were nearly out of the house when he told me about this, but I immediately started one myself. I could have thought it was too late, but I didn't care. I wanted something like this to hand down. No, it won't be the most read book on the shelf, and they may not even look at it until they're forty. But even when they're older, they'll appreciate what I've done.

It's not too late for you to start one, either. It's tough to find an empty journal big enough to put 365 entries in, so you may have to buy two. Spend the thirty dollars and do it. You won't regret it. Put a date on each page, and then when you make an entry, just mark the year. If you keep it by your favorite chair, you'll have an easier time remembering to write in it consistently.

One Picture Is Worth . . .

Go through the family photo albums with your son and pick out some of the best pictures of you two together. Make one big, framed montage for his room, and one for your office or den. Do this about every year or two and keep adding to the collection. Don't worry about creating empty panels in the photo albums. You don't look in them often enough for anyone to notice anyway. Get those pictures up on the wall where you both can look at them and smile and say, "Remember this one when we . . . ?"

Another option is to get the little binder photo albums, the type with one photo on each side of the pages, and have an ongoing book you can always look at. You'll end up making several if you keep them up—and you should keep them up! Then when he goes away to college, he'll have something to take with him.

Gifts to Last

One Christmas I made a wall hanging of each of my sons' favorite sports. Drew got karate. In an eight-and-a-half-by-eleven-inch frame I placed as many postage stamps from around the world I could find that had the sport on it. (Being a stamp collector, I had many of them, but then I went to a stamp store to find others. Some stores have a box of stamps marked "sports stamps.") I arranged them nicely, stuck them to a colored piece of paper, then put a little square note at the bottom that said, "To Drew from Dad, Christmas 1996." Troy's had a soccer theme. They're oft-neglected pieces of wall coverings now, but ten or twenty years from now they will evoke a smile and maybe a tear when my sons think that Dad did this just for them.

Lifetime relational bonding is the key. Do you see it?

One year Drew got interested in the stars and planets and such. I took my Christmas bonus and bought a pretty neat telescope. Together we learned how to look at the moon and Mars and Venus and the Halle Boop comet. For a few hundred bucks we spent hours together outside trying to find an American flag planted on the moon (which we never did find, surprisingly enough). Sure, he grew out of it, but he has the telescope now that he'll use with his kids one day while telling stories of him and grandpa.

Scrapbooking

When I was seven, I put together this scrapbook of pictures from old *Life* and *Look* magazines. It has cars from 1964, some Vietnam War photos, John F. Kennedy photos (with all the lips colored red . . . hmm), the Beatles, Pope Paul VI (I have no idea how that got in there, because we weren't Catholic), and tons of other period photos. It's an absolute hoot to look at. Does your son have a scrapbook of any type? If not, go get one tomorrow, have him cut things out from magazines or the newspaper, and let him create his own.

If I had it to do over again, every Christmas vacation I'd let my boys buy five or so magazines (that were clean) and have them cut them up and create a scrapbook for every year. (Dang, I wish I'd done that.)

14. *Doing Things He'll Never Forget*

Okay, now you're on a roll with these "unforgettable" themes. You have ideas for memories, ideas for things to build for your son, and now all you need is some lifetime "shared things" you can do and good ideas he can repeat with his own family.

Hobbies Together

Have you found things you two can do together by the hour? I collected stamps and coins and almost anything I could while growing up. (I was a high-percentage Beaver, remember?) I had hoped my sons would enjoy the same things. Alas, neither of them caught the stamp or coin bug. But they loved sports cards. The result: boxes and boxes of cards in the basement. Card shows, collecting autographs—all became the stuff of evenings and weekends together.

Besides all the outdoor games I played with my boys—soccer, baseball, football, basketball—they each had some favorite indoor games that they still like today: pool, cribbage, gin rummy, and of course video games.

Video games, as much as I liked them when they first came out (Pong, Pac-Man, and so on), suddenly got real complicated.

The control device was a few levels past my intelligence grade, and to be any good at them, you just had to play and play for hours. I have to admit that I failed as a dad at Video Games 101. I would get them for my boys but I'd only watch. It became more of something they did with their friends or when they needed to veg away from me. I tried a few Bible video games and I tried getting them hooked on a few of the old-time games I used to play, but to no avail. If I had it to do over again, I think I would buy more educational video games and get involved with my sons while playing them.

If you hunt or fish, you likely have a perfect hobby to spend hours of the best quality time you can with your son. The preparation of getting everything ready for the trip, the drive to the destination, the actual hunt for the fish and game, the stories you can tell afterward—there are really very few memories that compare for a young man than spending hours and days with Dad doing something so "manly."

With my own sons during those years we never hunted and we only fished a couple of times a year. There were simply too many soccer and baseball tourneys to attend in far-away cities and states. These were fine, but it was a lot of spectating while they competed, instead of teaching them new things. I regret that.

Making Your Home Party Central

A little-known way of keeping your relationship with your son strong is to make your home a place he is never embarrassed about inviting his friends over to. Mom will have to help with this some, naturally, but Dad, you can set the tone. When I was in youth ministry, I remember working with teens who would never invite me over to their house, because they were ashamed of how it looked, they were ashamed of their weird parents, or there was nothing to do there except watch TV. If you can possibly arrange it, what you need is a place to have games, foosball, food, and a private place for your kids to go with their friends. They'll reemerge when they're hungry; then you can be the hero and make milk shakes or smoothies or your special concoction of four cereals combined into one bowl that must have ice-cold milk added to make it perfect for human consumption.

You don't want to go overboard-goofy with your son's friends around, but a little controlled craziness for a short period of time says, "Dad's cool in small doses." Jokes? They'd better be good; otherwise forget it. And no showing them your high school fruit fly collection, either. And please don't outdo them with armpit flatulence. Yes, I know it's your spiritual gift, but save it for that one "special moment" where it'll be cool to look stupid. (Read: *one* moment.) As for real flatulence, well, that's a memory that you don't want your son's friends to have about you . . . unless you want it known by half the world.

Goofy Stuff

Sometimes a dad must step out of character and just do crazy things with his son, things he wouldn't want anyone else to know about.

Remember the Ernest movies? About twice a year I'd rent a couple of them and we'd go down in the basement— without Mom around—and eat pizza and watch Jim Varney in *Ernest Scared Stupid* or *Ernest Saves Christmas* or something equally moronic. But it was a blast and my guess is, my sons will make their sons do the same.

Whether it's midnight bowling on a weeknight (school night?), TP-ing Mom's car in the garage after she's gone to bed, skinny-dipping in a mountain lake (I didn't do this one), making peanut butter and jelly milk shakes (milk, then ice cream, then jelly, *then* the peanut butter), or using Mom's eyeliner to paint beards, mustaches, and sideburns on each other (and taking *lots* of pictures)—earn your Ph.D. in goofy and you'll have bonding memories for life. There's a good chance your son will recall these memories when he's angry at you for taking the car keys away a few years later. And while he'll act like an immature adolescent when you do (since this is what he is, count on him acting like that), because you've loaded up a bank vault of great times, he'll be more forgiving.

Expand His Horizons

Are you stuck in the same ol' same ol'? Practices, games, homework, video games, Blockbuster rentals, and pizza nights may be predictable and easy, but they don't often make for bonding or teachable moments. Here are a few ideas to try when you're in the mood to shake things up a little.

- Go see a play. Whether it's a local, small-time performance or a big-city theatrical (expensive) one, go do it.
- Attend Christian concerts. (This ought to be a family habit.)
- Take a woodworking class together and make something that will be around for a hundred years.
- Learn an instrument with your son. Both my boys took up a horn of some sort during their grade school years, but they lost interest in a short amount of time. I bet if I had done it with them, they wouldn't have quit so easily.
- Take voice lessons. That's right, you go with him and embarrass yourself right alongside him. For a guy especially, this could give him the confidence to join choirs

and the like or at a minimum sing songs a bit more robustly in church. He'll learn the breathing techniques necessary to carry a note longer than two beats. (Hey, and he might become a world-famous Christian singer who will make enough dough to ensure that you'll be in a nice assisted-living facility when you can't remember your name anymore.)

- Go to a couple of art galleries, then buy some paint-by-number masterpieces to work on together. And don't forget to frame them with some writing on the back telling when and where they were created. Then, after your son has mastered the numbers, see if he has the ability to paint the backyard (on a canvas ... the scenery). How about a portrait of the family pet?

- Take a pottery class. They aren't just for women (and if you're a single dad, I think it might be a great place to meet someone).

- Teach your son auto mechanics. It's never too early to begin. Thirty minutes a week learning about something new under the hood might give him a lifetime career. (Auto mechanics are in very short supply these days.) You could get free oil changes for life if you play your cards right.

- Start taking dance classes and ... nah, never mind. (Having three left feet, I know why dance really *is* of the Devil.)

- Learn how to make stained glass. Wouldn't that be cool? You'd be the only guy any of your friends or family members know who can do it. Just think of all the Christmas presents you could make on the cheap. You'd save enough to get that bass boat before your son graduates from college. And if you made lures out of stained glass, you might get your own Saturday morning TV show (and how many of your friends have one of those?). Then again, you might just make a lot of fish mad at you while they swim away with a cut lip. Maybe it's just a garage thing you do in November.

Your Memory Box

If you got out your old grade school memory stuff, you could come down to your son's level, if only for a short while. I have old ticket stubs, newspaper clippings of the baseball stars I idolized, GI Joe dog tags, a Cub Scout flashlight, a pocketknife from my visit to Canada, not to mention my old grade school pictures. Talk about a hilarious two hours together! He'll get bored, so don't drag it out too often.

Treasure Hunts

Do you travel in your work? I had to travel some when my sons were growing up, and when they were in grade school, I'd hide these little notes all over the house. Cards like:

"Hugs and kisses from Dad. Be home soon."
"Everyone get together and give each other a big hug. Wish I were there."
"Pray for Dad. He's praying for you."
"Time to give Mom a *big hug* and say thanks for taking such good care of us."
"Everyone give Drew a big hug and kiss and say, 'This is from Dad.'"
"This is just a small reminder that Dad loves his family *very much*. I am thinking about you."

Other types of treasure hunts led them to real treasure: little presents or envelopes full of quarters or candy or sports cards. Anything that would be a treasure for your son will be more fun for him if he finds it by going from one clue to the next. Will he remember these treasure hunts when he's older? Count on it!

Crazy Contests

Boys love to compete (some overly so), so why not do things they can win at? Why not do activities that don't matter who wins? Try these.

- Have you taught your son how to blow a bubble yet?
- Who can eat the most _____?
- How long can you hold your breath?
- Who can stare down the other?
- Who can pitch a penny closer to the wall?

Guy Flicks

Because you're sometimes pretty tired on evenings or weekends, you just can't do much more than sit on the couch and watch a good movie. You've had a long week, a long day, whatever; just get a good movie, pop some popcorn, and warm up the VCR. Here are some pretty good dad-son movies:

Hoosiers—commitment to a team, listening to coaches, confidence

Gettysburg*—history of our country's fight for freedom

The Patriot*—the importance of family in the face of adversity

Apollo 13—how good things can happen in spite of bad circumstances

Rudy—persistence pays off

Forrest Gump*—acceptance of others
The Sandlot—belonging, friendship, acceptance of others
Mr. Holland's Opus—bearing fruit
Angels in the Outfield—believing in something
The Truman Show—character
The Karate Kid—diligence
Indiana Jones and the Last Crusade*—doubt and faith
Toy Story—envy
Hook—the importance of family
The Princess Bride—this is just a fun movie
Willy Wonka and the Chocolate Factory—greed and glut-
    tony
A Time to Kill*—race issues
That Thing You Do—relationships and self-worth
Chariots of Fire—standing up for what you believe
Independence Day—overcoming evil
October Sky—heroes
The Prince of Egypt—becoming what God created you to
    be
Simon Birch—how God uses people
Toy Story 2—stealing
What About Bob?—mercy
Frequency*—communication, relationships

* Some scenes in this movie will not be appropriate for
younger children.

Resources:

Fields, Doug, and Eddie James. *Videos That Teach 1*.
    Grand Rapids: Zondervan, 1999.
Fields, Doug, and Eddie James. *Videos That Teach 2*. Grand
    Rapids: Zondervan, 2001.

DeMoss, Bob. *The Great TV Turnoff.* Westchester, Ill.: Crossway, 2001.

Dad-Son Getaways

Drew was just nine when he and I boarded a plane and went to see my ailing mother. A buddy of mine was a book designer, and I asked if he would take an empty book and put a cover on it that said, "Drew and Dad's Wacky Adventure." It was bright yellow with an airplane illustration on the cover. It served as both photo album and journal. He wrote in it, as did I. We chronicled everything we did: what food we ate, what kinds of planes we flew in, locations where we landed, and games we played. (He got a twenty-eight in cribbage his very first game!) It was a four-day lifetime memory that now has a book we wrote together to remind him that dads and sons spend time doing things they'll remember forever. (When he was fifteen, we went to London and Paris together, continuing the tradition.)

If you have more than one son, don't always try to kill two birds with one stone. Do these types of things individually with each son so they have unique memories.

Going on a TV and Computer Fast

Nothing can monopolize a dad and son's time any more than TV and the computer. My own proclivity to spend "quality" time in front of the tube simply watching endless Rambo movies isn't something I'm proud of. What I did was to sparingly go on "fasts" of both TV and the computer. We'd read, go out and do something fun, or just find other ways to keep ourselves occupied so the central focus of our time wasn't the idiot screens in our lives.

How long should a fast be? Start with one or two days and work your way up to a week or a month, if you dare. Like you, I know several families who don't even own a TV, and for the most part they have kids who haven't turned out too bad.

Don't be afraid to do something out of the ordinary like a TV fast. It will force you to try new things, not to mention carry on actual conversations about subjects besides how many home runs Barry Bonds will hit or how many free throws Shaq will miss.

Normal Fun Sports That You Do Together

While I've mentioned sports several times, there are some sports and activities that truly foster a great relationship better than others. What you want is to do things that give you and your son times of fun and adventure but also times to talk and just relax sitting next to each other. What sports do this? Downhill skiing, cross-country skiing, ice fishing, fishing and hunting trips (Dr. Dobson still talks about his days hunting with his own dad as the best times of his life), hiking, mountain climbing, and rock climbing, to name a few.

Spectator sports aren't bad, either. While major-league baseball games can be fun to attend, going to minor-league parks and participating in all the fan-involvement stuff that goes on—not to mention having the chance to be close to the action—is a perfect way to spend time together and create great memories. At our own Sky Sox Stadium, each game we'd put our name in the box for drawings, prizes, and contests. Troy got selected once to get dizzy at home plate by running around a bat ten times, then trying to run to second base. He won the race against another kid and won a video and free tickets to a later game. When Drew was seven, he got selected to throw a beanbag through one of three small holes in a piece of plywood. He hit the second smallest target and won a fifty-dollar bill! Tell me he won't remember that the rest of his life.

We've been to spring training in Arizona a couple of times to watch the big leaguers up close. At major-league parks you have to be extremely lucky to get an autograph, but at these low-key games most of the players sign everything put in front of them. Some will even consent to having their pictures taken with fans. Actual conversations break out between little boys and their great big heroes.

I have friends who have taken their sons to preseason football workouts (college and pro), to watch professional skaters train at our World Arena, even to high school sports events.

What sports are fun to do in small doses that will give you some great memories? Paintball wars, laser tag, bowling, archery, Frisbee golf, regular golf or simply hitting a bucket or two of golf balls. The key is variety and consistency. Make as many thoughts of Dad as possible be associated with fun times.

Games

What else should you keep going from your son's childhood years?

Believe it or not—games.

Find a game that belongs to the two of you. As much as I wanted it to be cribbage or Careers, my youngest son and I settled on chess. The reason? He can beat me about half the time. I love it! When you pick a game that your son loses at every time, he'll get tired of it. Develop a one-on-one game so when your son comes back from college or his own family, there will be only one choice as to what to do together. And remember, it's not the competition but the fellowship you're after.

The same is true for a family game. You want to help your son take the traditions you started and carry them over into his family (though it is hopefully years away). If you neglect the little things like games during his teen years, the traditions aren't quite as solidified. He'll have grade school memories, then nothing.

That One Thing That Is *Your* Thing

Hobbies will change as the years go by, so it's not necessary to develop one hobby you do together. The key is to always have something fun you both love. What my son Drew and I did when he was twelve was to create Bible word searches. We'd pick a topic like the twelve tribes, famous kings, minor prophets, the twelve apostles, cities mentioned in the book of Acts, parables, key words, whatever, and create a word search. They didn't have to be big, honking word searches; the small ones worked fine. We also did sports teams, famous home run hitters, even sportscasters. (Yes, we were a little too much of a sports family.) Not only did we create a book full of word searches, but we had something we'll keep forever. And I am certain of one thing: he'll do it with his kids later in life.

Once my oldest got his license, our hours together were never the same. Yet I also knew that few things were more essential than extended time together. We never fished much because of his year-round sports schedule. We weren't hunters or hikers but we both loved basketball. Starting in grade school and ending his junior year, each March we drove to Denver to see the state championships, sometimes even getting a motel room instead of driving home. One of the most memorable times for both of us was when he ate too much greasy food during the first two games of the day. He felt sick and didn't want to stay for the 5-A championship game, so we left early, got a room . . . and he proceeded to throw up for about an hour. Eventful, memorable, bonding. A lifetime memory.

Whether it's daylong trips skiing, hiking, or fishing, try to find something that allows you and your son to spend hours together. Topics of discussion will come up that never would have in the day-to-day rush of homework, practices, and work.

The main thing is, don't give up. Just because your son is a teenager doesn't mean your focused time of relational bonding is over. If anything, those years are the ones in which to turn up the heat a little and be more proactive. If you let the daily grind overpower what's most important, you'll become one of those "If only . . ." parents I've talked to so many times:

"If only I would have dated my son more."
"If only I wouldn't have been afraid of my son's chang-ing, more moody behavior."

And when they get to college, you'll say, "If only I could go back to being the human cash machine instead of the human Ben Franklin machine."

15. Teaching Things He'll Never Forget

While memories and hobbies and all are good ends in and of themselves, many of the things you'll do with your son will lead to perfect introductions to talk about anything and everything. Don't let these unique bonding times get away from you. Take the initiative; then, as appropriate, bring up things about life and faith you want him to never forget.

Raising the Perfect Gentleman

I'll never forget the time my dad taught me how to shake hands firmly with men (and the difference in a handshake with a woman) and to stand when a lady enters the room. He was very intentional about the gentlemanly graces. Just because you didn't learn these things until you were out of college doesn't mean you wait until your son is twenty before teaching him about holding silverware correctly, placing napkins in the lap, and how to address women of different ages and marital status ("See that ring on her left hand, Son? That means she's a 'Ma'am,' not a 'Miss' or a 'Ms.'").

Do you want him to get married one day and treat his wife like a queen (as you do)? Then treat your bride as if she were queen of all queens. "Please." "Thank you." "Can I help?" (Go ahead, say it. I know you can.) "Here, let me do that." Reward him in secret for every gentlemanly act you see. That's right, cash money. He'll learn better and that payment habit won't be hard to break (because you and I both know that quarters will soon become insulting . . . and you'll never give him dollars).

The point is to make him more couth than you are, so he has a chance to impress quality girls instead of getting lucky, as you did. He'll thank you for it later.

Mr. Entrepreneur

My grade school years were filled with ways to make some pocket change. I built a putt-putt course in the dirt in my backyard and charged the neighbor kids a dime each to play. I think I made eighty cents before rain washed mud into the holes. Garage sales? I had them all the time. I sold my dad's high school baseball mitt for a buck. (I think he had to buy it back for three bucks.) I was always asking Mom and Dad what I could sell.

Take the hobby you've landed on together and use it to make some money. Christmas ornaments are a natural, as are lawn doodads, picture frames, little wall-mounted boxes that moms can put knickknacks in—there are literally hundreds of things that you and your son can make together.

By giving him the encouragement he needs to start a lawn mowing service in the neighborhood, you will save tons of movie rental and burger money. Can he rake leaves? Shovel snow? Walk a dog? Pull weeds? If you give him the knowledge that "hard work brings a profit" (Proverbs 14:23), you could save yourself the heartache you would suffer years later when you wind up with a lazy son because it was easier for you to be the human cash machine. But he needs to know what to do, how to do it, what to charge, and how to market it. You know all this stuff, right, Dad? Start this weekend.

Exercising for Fun and Profit

I'm an ex-jock, so I'm not grossly out of shape or overweight, but I have found that life has become busy enough that it's tough for me to find time for consistent exercise. I've tried several contraptions designed to make me burn calories, and some I've actually used for more than a week or two. But what would keep me consistent above anything I've tried before is to find something my son and I could do together. Walking, jogging, going to a fitness place for some weightlifting (the best thing, I believe, a dad and son can do together), whatever—experiment and find exercise stuff you and your son can do together.

Handling Money

Want to get your son's attention real quick? Tell him you're going to teach him the art of money management, but you realize he must have some actual money to manage, so you're going to double his allowance. Knowing how to track expenses, give to the Lord, understand compound interest, and appreciate the value of saving money will yield lifetime fruit. You may want to wait until he's on the older side of his preteen years, but sound money management is an acquired skill, not something he'll learn by osmosis. The best part is, it puts you two together to talk about something he's likely motivated to learn. Larry Burkett's organization, Crown Financial Ministries, has several resources for teaching kids about money; they can be found at your local Christian bookstore or by logging on to crown.org.

Friendship Skills

Most boys don't struggle with making or keeping friends. The struggle is in finding the right ones to hang out with. This isn't as essential in the grade school years but becomes very essential during the early teen years. If you wait until your son is thirteen before you make this issue a priority, however, by then he may have developed some bad habits. This is one skill that is best taught through asking the right questions.

"What do you look for in a friend?"

"How would you know if a friend wasn't being a good friend?"

"In what ways are you a good friend to your buddies?"

"What are some things friends shouldn't do to other friends?"

"Do you have enough friends?"

"Why don't some people have more friends?"

"How do you make friends of strangers?"

"Is there someone at school who's a loner whom you could be friends with?"

These types of questions are thinking points for him on an important topic. The Scripture is true: "Bad company corrupts good character" (1 Corinthians 15:33). So you need to be diligent to not let your son's friends tear down the moral foundation you're trying to build. Once the teen years arrive, this will be the bane of your existence. That once fresh-faced little cherub will soon be hearing—and listening—to other voices who whisper patent untruths into his virgin ears.

Believe it or not, the primary weapon to combat these negative influences isn't to put him in an unreal "Christian" environment. If he is forearmed in the art of choosing and developing good friends, he will make his own right choices without you having to be there. And that's what you want anyway. You don't want to have to monitor everything in his life; rather you want him to self-monitor his behavior when he's alone and when he's with friends.

Make a Top-100 List

Okay, you're a perceptive dad, right? What are the one hundred things that you want your son to learn and that you can teach him during his teenage years to prepare him for life? Start making that list now so you can begin to check them off. Those years between eighth grade and senior year absolutely fly by. Whoosh! Gone. All too soon he'll be out the door, only to return when he needs to eat or sleep or bum gas money. It's happened to me—twice! Though I thought I did a pretty good job along the way, I still find myself playing catch-up a little on things I forgot to teach. Teaching him to change a tire before he leaves home, for example, may save you a hundred dollar towing bill ($115 to be exact).

16. Finding People He'll Never Forget

While you, Dad, are the one your son will always remember the most, I hope you sense the need to make sure that other adults have input into his life. This is one of the big keys to his maturity as a man and as a follower of Christ.

Adult Friends

Neither of my boys had grandparents who were actively involved in their lives during the eight- to twelve-year-old years. My parents had died while my sons were small, and because we had moved so often, my wife's parents were a thousand miles away. I'm a bit heartsick about this. My sons would have benefited from getting away from Mom and Dad more often and spending time with their grandparents (as my wife and I would have benefited from having more time alone). The few times they did spend time with them were wonderful. My oldest son caught his first fish with his grandpa near the same spot on the McKenzie River in Oregon where I caught my first fish with my grandpa. I was the only one to catch a fish that day in 1966, and so was he in 1991!

Not having grandparents close by isn't all that unusual these days, sad to say. So in order for your boy not to miss out on what other adults can teach him, you have to be intentional and creative in finding other men who live and model the same ideals you have.

Scouting might be the best. Again, because my sons' sports dance card was always full, this was an impossibility for them. But if your son only plays one sport or doesn't play any, it's absolutely something you should do. To enumerate the benefits of three to eight years of scouting isn't necessary. With the right leaders it could be the best investment in your son's maturity you could ever make.

On occasion I would have the privilege of having missionaries or speakers in our home. I always told the visitor beforehand that I would be asking them questions about how they came to faith or about what miracles they saw God doing in their work, so my boys could hear from someone else besides me about the neat things God does. Again, I wish I would have done this even more. Those are things that young minds just don't forget. Besides, it opened up to them the world of ministry that I hoped they would consider as their life's work.

We befriended several other families like ours in which all the children were boys. And when I say "befriended," I mean that a couple of them became real family to us. Meals and holidays together, not to mention frequent vacations and outings, all proved to pay dividends as my sons grew through their teen years. Parents often become the invisible aliens as boys enter their teen years, but because there were other adults with a lot of history with my boys, they could check in with my sons on their walk with God or on their future plans almost as well as I could. And I was able to do the same with many of my sons' friends. Because of my background of growing up in a single-parent household, I often took on the role of a surrogate dad for boys whose fathers weren't involved much. But building strong adult relationships doesn't start in the teenage years. You have to build up a few fun preparatory years in late grade school to help cement the relationship by giving you some history with them.

Being a student of teenagers as I've been for so long, I've discovered that one major area of neglect is the connection with the older generation. In previous decades extended families didn't have entire states separating them; people stayed close to parents, grandparents, and sometimes great-aunts and great-uncles. Roots are essential to long-term relationships. That sense of connectedness with older family members somehow ties the heart to the family name and heritage. Not every boy will respond to taking much time with the older set, because, well, they're old and boring (or so they think).

Though my parents and grandparents have been long gone, I have a widowed great-uncle who has hung around for ninety-plus years. He served in World War II, fixing B-17s in Italy. He still has his uniform and Army Air Corps medals. And before he started losing his memory, he had tons of stories. I made sure my boys spent time with him when we'd visit his one-bedroom Portland, Oregon, home he bought after the war (and lived in for fifty-five years!). He's the family's only connection to the past, and like it or not, one day they're going to appreciate that they knew someone who was in the Second World War.

Though it may be painful for a moment, go ahead and force your boy to take time with as many of your old extended family members as you can. Even if his only memory is that Great-Aunt Connie didn't even have a VCR, he will one day realize there is history to his family name.

Grandparenting Near and Far

All this said, a dad cannot downplay the importance of grandparents in a son's life. It's connection to the family history, to be sure, but it can be much more than that, especially during that all-essential eight- to twelve-year-old range (before he becomes a teenager and suddenly knows everything).

Let's first admit that some of us don't necessarily want our kids to have too much exposure to our parents or our wife's parents. They were perhaps clueless parents themselves, so why give them a chance to mess up another generation? And if our parents weren't all that good, they probably aren't that motivated to be involved grandparents. If this is the case, you're in the clear. You can do occasional holidays and vacations with minimal damage.

But if you don't know by now, most grandparents have lived for the day to be grandparents. If your son has any like these, and if they are also good people, you have much needed allies in the long-term goal of solidifying the family relationship for life. And if your relationship with your son's grandparents is good, all the better. You're in a position to take full advantage of a wonderful situation.

My next suggestion may seem like a weird one, but since you're reading this book and thus not flying by the seat of your pants in parenting your son, why not clue in the grandparents about some of your plans as you prepare for the teenage years? Here's how you do it: Get them alone, away from your son, and say something like, "First of all, I want to thank you for being such good parents (talk from your heart as honestly as you can). Second, it's not going to be an easy proposition to raise this son (include your daughter if you have one) through his teenage years. My goal as a dad (as parents) is to guide him toward the Lord and toward being a functioning adult. What I teach him about God and good behavior is really important, but even more important is my relationship with him. He's going to mess up along the way, as I did, but if our relationship is strong, then when he malfunctions, he'll always know he has a place to come back to. Third, you can really help."

This is where you tell them how essential you see their role to be. "I'm not looking for parenting advice, though if you see something really wacky about what I'm doing, you can mention it. What I'd love is for you to spend as much time as you can with him, as much as your schedule allows, to say the same things in your own way that I'm saying about the Lord, life, and the importance of character. Sometimes kids can talk about things with their grandparents that they can't with their parents—if the relationship is strong. So I want your relationship with them to be strong."

If the grandparents don't keel over from a heart attack at this point, you can then discuss how you and they can work together to accomplish this goal. Here are a few suggestions.

- Start with short intervals of fun and busy things. Don't send your son away for a weekend or a week unless he's already used to it and likes it. Give him time to discover that spending time with his grandparents is cool. He will likely hit it off with his grandpa more than with his grandma, so just talk about this reality up front without discouraging her. She'll likely be more creative than his grandpa anyway, so it will probably work out fine.

- Rather than having Grandpa try to learn video games, emphasize how great it would be if he and your son could develop a few things that are special to just them. Fishing, woodworking, hiking, collecting something, going to minor-league baseball games—anything that puts them together for long stretches of time. That's where relationships are really solidified.

- Give your parents permission to tell stories about you. No, maybe not *every* story, but sometimes a son has the mistaken notion that his dad was somehow perfect growing up. Because you've had some years to chip away at the rough edges, you're a lot more perfect now than you used to be (and have learned to hide most of the imperfections). Grandmas will tell stories better than grandpas because their memory is better. "Do you want to hear a story about your dad?" will be a great opening line in the course of doing something together. There's a power in storytelling that sermonizing just can't match. The listener is suddenly tied emotionally to the person in the story. Whether it's a funny story or a serious one, your son will have more reason to see you as a fellow struggler rather than as Mr. Perfect. (And the reason why you want this is the same reason why God didn't stay in heaven. He became Immanuel—God with us—so we could see him for ourselves. Yes, he was perfect when he came down to earth, but because he was also a man who struggled with temptation, he is able to help those who struggle.)

- Let the grandparents know that consistent little things count more than the big things. Large birthday checks or trips to Disneyland are important, but it's often the constant contact that binds the relationship. Cards, phone calls, emails, handwritten letters, and small gifts make more of a long-term statement than the occasional big stuff. This is especially true if the grandparents don't live nearby.

- The goal for Grandpa during the eight- to twelve-year-old range is to have fun with your son and build that bank vault of great memories, not to help him solve his girl problems or make him a grade school "super-Christian." By making things special between those two, if trouble hits later, your son has a place to go to spend time, and someone with whom to discuss life questions.

- The grandparents mustn't be concerned about "character correction." They're not the parent, you are. Their goal is to be best buds and leave you the task of parenting.

- Encourage lots of photos of your son and his grandpa, and your son and his grandma. This shouldn't be too hard to do, given that you can't even become a grandparent unless you have a minimum of two cameras and a camcorder on your person at all times. This way the grandparents can create individual photo albums filled with pictures of themselves and their grandson to give him later in life. (Just as you're doing, right?)

- Give the grandparents permission to be over-the-top diligent in staying in touch, even when your son is going through his various adolescent phases. I think some grandparents would get discouraged if their grandson all of a sudden became moody or disinterested in spending time with them. Tell them it will likely happen, but not to lose heart. They're essential to your son's long-term emotional and spiritual health, so they can't give up. Perseverance will have a payoff when the kid goes to college and has *really* broken away from his parents. He'll need a place to land with questions and connection as never before. By relationally sowing in the easy grade school years and being persistent through the tough teenage years—together as parent and grandparent—the harvest of a healthy adult will be had.

By being diligent yourself in enlisting a few allies in the battle for your son's heart, you've given him more reasons to stay connected to the place where God's love—through people whom he loves—can always reach him.

Prayer Warriors

When our boys hit the teenage years, Elaine and I became evangelistic proponents of praying together for each one's current needs, immediate future, and big things like college choice, career path, and future wife. We would pray separately, naturally, but we developed the habit (through the diligence of my wife) of four to five times a week praying for our boys. We'd do it at the same time every day—right before I'd go to work.

Though it is hard to measure the direct effect this has had, I would not want to go through the parenting years without this discipline. We've seen such miracles in our sons' lives, but even more so we've seen miracles in our own faith as we've continually given our boys back to God for his protection. This is a lifetime habit that I am convinced we will never lose.

Just as it's a boy's responsibility to develop his own faith, it is God's responsibility to draw each child to himself. And this must be our prayer at all times. My wife and I have been fortunate to also have the prayers of others along the way.

Elaine's grandma was in constant prayer for our two sons. We have friends whose sons we pray for and they pray for ours. We believe in the power of prayer and are not bashful about asking others to intercede for our boys.

Find a few prayer partners who will not let heaven rest until your son knows the Lord and is following him closely.

Part Five:

Imparting Spiritual Truths

17. Eternal Values

While much of this book has ideas and thoughts about imparting spiritual values, there comes a time when you have to be intentional about teaching spiritual disciplines you want your son to have for a lifetime. And late grade school is not too early to do it. In fact, it's likely the best time to do it. Why? Remember, your son still pretty much likes you a lot. Further, he isn't as stained by the world as he may be later in adolescence. So . . . what's the goal?

My goal was to make sure my sons knew that their relationship with God was *their* relationship with God. While it's natural for your son to borrow your faith (since he'll be borrowing everything else for many years to come), no one gets into heaven on his parents' coattails. The earlier he knows this, the better. If you're from an evangelical home, my guess is that your son has "prayed the salvation prayer." Good. Great. Wonderful. Fantastic. But since nearly every kid does this before age six, you'd better be aware that young hearts have a tendency to drift far away from God. Satan is persistent and patient and is not averse to taking a childlike faith and turning it into adultlike fear or unbelief.

True confessions time. Our youngest prayed the prayer and has yet to waver. He's been a dad's dream child. He's diligent with his faith on his own, has kept his behavior pure, and likes to read his Bible and learn more about God. I was the perfect dad, right? Wrong. Our oldest son prayed the prayer too, but from age eleven or so was basically disinterested in God beyond making sure he was going to heaven. He had a lot of athletic skills, he got lots of strokes from it, he had a measure of popularity, his dad had dough.... Life was easy enough that he didn't see a need for God for quite some time. We sent him off to college not really being one hundred percent sure which direction he'd go should the plane go down. And that's about the most uncomfortable feeling a Christian parent can have. It brought my wife and me to our knees on a regular basis (so that was good), but we had no way of knowing when he'd finally sense his own need for God.

The story has a happy ending, as late in his freshman year of college he did make that choice to trust his life to the Savior. The great thing about the wait was that it was his choice, in his way and God's time.

It's hard to realize, but your son may not be on the "do it while you're young and really mean it" timetable. In fact, my experience has been that only about one-third of boys are on this sort of timetable. The rest are going to test your patience, test your own trust in God's timing, and test what the world has to offer first before they come to the realization that they need Jesus Christ for their very own.

That's why the principles and ideas in this book need to be given more than a passing glance. If a son takes his time before he finally gets it, then when he does get it, he must have a place to come home to. He must have other people, including you, to tell his story to. When Troy finally made his decision for Christ, we weren't the first people he called. It was a family friend who had invested time in talking to him and praying for him whom he called at 2:00 a.m. Why? Because she (another mom) told him that after he did it, he had to call her first!

While it may hurt your pride as a pillar of a Christian dad to think that you can't lead your own son to the Lord before he leaves home, get over yourself. You can't. It's God's job to draw your son to himself at your son's appointed hour. And if God performs this big miracle, you can count on him to do what it takes to keep your son strong in the faith for his entire life. Isn't this what you want anyway? We had a saying in Youth for Christ when I was a Campus Life director: "If you save him, you have to keep him. If God saves him, it's *his* job to keep him." That kept us from having pride in how many people we were winning to Christ, and it gave God permission to draw whomever he wanted, whenever he wanted, however he wanted. It was God, then, who had to help them—partly through our persistent discipling—to work out their salvation over the long haul.

I hope none of these realities dissuade you from doing your due diligence today with your preteen son. While God will save and grow your son in his own way and in his own time, it's very nerve-racking to wait for that process to yield the fruit you want. It's better to give it as many nudges as you possibly can.

So where do you start? The next chapter tells you exactly where the starting point begins—with you!

18. Congratulations, You're a Theology Professor!

Not a day goes by that you and I aren't required to teach. Let's take a quick inventory of all the subjects: cooking, home maintenance, auto repair, personal hygiene, etiquette, time management, interpersonal relationships, computer science, bicycle upkeep, yard enhancement, fundraising (being a salesman), minor health care, organization, how to quarter a buck two miles from camp, how to filet a catfish, and let's not forget the art of running a post pattern in the backyard without trampling a sprinkler head. And if you broke each of these subjects down to their basic elements, the list would be endless. I guess that's why God gives us at least eighteen years with our sons before they leave the nest.

Teaching these essential life skills are part of the job we accepted when signing on as a dad. I tended to teach these skills the same way they were taught to me—which means my boys will know how to make their yard look good, but they'd better learn their car maintenance and repair from auto shop at school. I can teach them a lot, but showing them the intricacies of the inside of an engine is the perfect way to convince them how mechanically impaired I really am.

But you knew all this already, didn't you? It's natural for a dad to try to teach his sons stuff they should know and do for themselves, so he won't have to do it for them later. As your son moves from stage to stage, you'll teach him all these essential subjects in the classroom of everyday life. And it'll be truly rewarding to see him pass most of these subjects with flying colors.

What about theology? Do you know that you are your son's theology professor too?

In Bible college I took three terms of both New Testament and Old Testament theology. Upper division courses. And since I didn't know what the word *theology* meant before I got to school, I was a little scared about what the classes might entail. Every junior or senior I talked to said they'd be the toughest classes I'd ever take (except Greek and Hebrew—which I didn't take). But since they were required for graduation, there was no escaping them.

Webster's defines *theology* as "the study of God and the relations between God and the universe; the study of religious doctrines and matters of divinity." That's a fairly accurate definition.

Did anyone ever tell you that this would be part of the lifelong job description of a dad? Read it again . . . think of your kids . . . ponder your qualifications . . . then forget about it and send your kids to Sunday school or a Christian school.

Dilemma solved, right?

Wrong!

Whether you like it or not, whether you're qualified or not, whether you *realize* it or not, you're the theology professor in your home (as is your wife, of course). Every day, every hour, you're teaching your child about God, the Bible, and the truth or falsehood of the Christian faith. And how well you do it will often—though not always—determine what type of Christian your son will turn out to be.

I'm sorry, but no resignations will be accepted at this point. Too late. You have a boy, you want to raise him to love God, you're a theology professor. End of discussion.

Five Essentials

Breathe easy for a minute, because you won't have to stand in front of the classroom of your home, try to get your son's attention for an hour a day, five days a week, pool your ignorance with your mate, and dole out spiritual truths as if you were Chuck Swindoll. You do, however, need to do some thinking about what you're already doing.

1. Am I Representing the God of the Bible?

There is never a truer word spoken than this: Your son will generally think about God the way he thinks about you.

Until he's older, it's tough for him to realize that God is a little better than you, a little more loving, forgiving, perfect, and so forth. It's simply too hard for your son to think, *Okay, my dad yells at me and grounds me when I really mess up, but God would never yell. His patience is long-suffering.* It doesn't work that way. If you're a yeller, God must be a yeller. If you are constantly emphasizing your son's behavior, God must be most concerned about behavior. If you punish beyond what the "crime" demands, God is probably worse.

Get the picture? The picture is, *you're* the picture. How accurately your life reflects the character of God often determines whether your child grasps the true character of God.

Do you know what I want my kids to say about me at my funeral (a long time from now)? "I knew what God was like by watching my dad. And that's why I chose to serve Jesus Christ my whole life. My father wasn't perfect, didn't pretend to be. But he lived in such a way that I was certain that God was someone I could always trust, who would always love me, and who would never give up on me."

If that's what I want to hear, I'd better teach this theology by the way I live and the way I treat my children.

2. Am I Showing My Son the True Nature of Man and God's Plan of Salvation through Jesus?

To the untrained eye, the God of the Old Testament and the God of the New Testament are two different Gods. In the Old Testament we see a God of judgment. He's a lawgiver and he expects a lot of laws to be obeyed—or else (which isn't unlike the way many fathers parent their sons). While we see glimpses and foreshadows of the New Testament God throughout the Old Testament, his true character isn't completely crystallized for us until we see the lengths this God will go to in order to show his love to his creation.

Most scholars agree that the Old Covenant simply set up the New Covenant, that we had to know the true depravity and hopelessness of our sin nature before we realized that our deepest need was for a Savior.

This is the dilemma for many boys growing up in churchgoing families. They don't have a sense of how much of a sinner they are (because usually their life is going pretty well), so why should they pursue a Savior? Naturally, some catch on, but for many it takes some months or years of feeding pigs before they come to their senses (a word picture from the story of the prodigal son in Luke 15).

Since I don't want my sons to have to feed pigs, I must model my own need for a Savior. That means that I can't act as if I were perfect, that I accept responsibility for my actions, and that my conversational prayers in front of my children reveal my thankfulness for Jesus and all he did. I want my boys to think, *Dad is always talking about his need for a Savior. Maybe I need one too.*

If I constantly model the right theology about who I am (a sinner) and who Jesus is (the Savior), my kids will have few doubts about the true Gospel. And that's one thing I want them to always understand.

3. Am I Helping My Son Gain an Appreciation and Love for the Body of Christ?

Perhaps more than ever before, boys are asking, "Why church?" I've asked myself that question many times. Like you, I've listened to and sung hymns and songs that are either banal or archaic. I've gone along with pastors who prayed prayers that had no power in their presentation or meaning regarding where I was at spiritually and emotionally on that particular day. Then of course there are the hundreds of sermons—good and "bad"—by my pastor and "special speakers." Plays and skits have been the best, and I'm always amazed at the special music. There must be a wonderful place in heaven for those who have the courage to sing in front of a crowd of people. (Hopefully, I'll get to visit.)

Our real dilemma is that what I've described in the preceding paragraph is the church *service*, not the body of Christ. If you and I have difficulty keeping the two distinct, imagine what our sons are going through. To nearly every boy, church is the service. Who's leading the music this week, who's speaking, how the sound system works, whether anyone says hi, how the offering is received—these factors determine our sons' attitude about church.

Should I mention that what we say at home about church leaves the greatest impression on our sons? (Nah. Too convicting.)

This one, Dad, we must be absolutely intentional about. We can't afford to hope our sons catch the real truth about the body of Christ. We have to place it firmly in their bread basket. Too many fathers are fumbling this handoff, and the church of the twenty-first century will be minus a generation of men because of it. Let me give you a few suggestions for consideration:

- Quit saying, "Time to go to church." Say, "Time to go to the worship service." Start making this subtle change now and it may stick in your son's head by the time he leaves the nest. He has to quit thinking that church is that sixty to ninety minutes on Sunday morning.

- Do some home Bible studies. Dust off the concordance to find, read, and discuss together as a family as many passages as you can on these subjects: the body of Christ, church, gathering or assembling, worship, fellowship, spiritual gifts.

- Invite a pastor or youth pastor to your home or out for a meal and ask them to address this important issue. An informal guest speaker will add weight to what you've talked about in the home.

What you'll likely conclude from all this is that the church is the instrument God has chosen to reach the world. Each Christian is a member of the worldwide body of Christ and has been specially chosen to use his or her gifts and talents to point others to the Savior. Without a conscious involvement in this body, we won't know what the "abundant life" is all about, because we find our life by giving it away.

Which leads to the fourth question you must ask.

4. Am I Giving My Son a Love for Serving Others?

Being filled is important. The weekly worship service, personal prayer, and Bible study are a must. But I heard something years ago that has stuck with me like few other sayings: "When you stop giving, you stop growing."

I once went twenty months without missing a day in the Word (and I have a quiet-time notebook to prove it). But I intentionally quit my streak one summer day because the streak was the goal, not serving. I felt very spiritual as I religiously read my Bible, but then I just started to feel fat. It's not that I wasn't serving during those many months. Actually, I was in full-time youth ministry in Youth for Christ. But when my eyes got focused—even ever so slightly—on a different goal, one that was certainly more quantifiable than the nebulous goal of serving, I found it too easy to mistake reading the Bible for being an active member of the body of Christ. Doing my daily spiritual duty did not equal abundant living.

True Christianity and true spirituality aren't just about observing our religious rituals. They're about giving our lives away. Just as Jesus did. He went about doing good. And if we want our teens to truly understand the purpose-filled abundant life, they must see us consistently being servants. Certainly, they'll eventually realize all that we did for them as parents (probably when they are parents themselves), but when they see us outside the home serving the poor, the homeless, our neighbors, our extended family, missionaries—anyone—they find the purpose in life they must have to make Jesus and the Christian faith real.

Serving is where it's at—and I didn't say anything about writing checks (because they'll rarely notice this, or rarely care when they do).

5. Is the Pursuit of Holiness a Noticeable Value in My Life?

This is a gigantic subject, worthy of reading many books about, so these few paragraphs are guaranteed not to do this essential Christian attribute justice. Needless to say, we're scared by the word *holiness*, awed by it, and often confused by it. We'd love to exemplify it more often, and we'd love it even more if our sons began their own personal search for its meaning and practice (for which of course we could take partial credit).

I'm at my holiest when I blow it in front of one of my boys. An innocuous swear word on the basketball court, undeserved sarcasm directed toward my wife, a half-truth to a phone solicitor during dinner—all these human foibles serve to bring me down to their level (though this is not my intent). And when I'm on their level, they see Jesus through me more clearly. The best thing God ever did for me was to become a human to show me what he was really like. Though Jesus led a perfect life, I can somehow touch him easier. God is not so far out of reach.

The first step to holiness is making it reachable, not necessarily attainable. Perfect holiness won't be fully grasped until we see Jesus face to face, for then we will be like him (1 John 3:2). Reachable holiness involves first recognizing our sinful humanity and understanding the true power of repentance.

Repentance, including the turning away from the sin that so easily entangles (Hebrews 12:1), is what moves us up the ladder of holiness. It's our lifetime job. It's the process of becoming more like Jesus. It's what makes being a Christian the toughest challenge we will ever have. It's the agony when we fail and the ecstasy when we confess and once again become clean before the Father. It's growing to appreciate the person of Jesus Christ more and more because Romans 7 really is true: I want to do right but I just can't. And then it's realizing that Romans 8:1–2 is even more true: I am not condemned because I am *in* Christ.

Well, I told you I couldn't do that word justice, and now I've proved it. Holiness means so much that it's hard to describe, even harder to live. But try to live it we must. For by living it, we are teaching it. And in the long term it may be the most important theological lesson we will ever pass on to our sons.

Being a theology professor is who you are, whether or not you like it or realize it. Every day you're representing God and teaching your son about him. What are some other essentials along the way? They all point to that one major theme of the whole book—relationships.

19. *It's the Relationship, Stupid*

Sorry, I didn't mean to call you stupid. But we dads *are* pretty stupid sometimes. We are so performance driven, we have a tendency to think that if God asked us the question, "How do you think I could start loving you more?" we'd say something like, "The more I do as a Christian, the more you'll love me."

Buzzzzz. Wrong answer! You lose fifty points.

Your relationship with God is about love and grace and realizing that you're simultaneously a no-good pig of a human being and God's most precious and wonderful creation—both at the same time. You know your heart is evil and can't be tamed (along with your tongue), but you also know that God doesn't grade on a curve. It's pass-fail, and because of Jesus you have passed!

Does your son know that?

Does everything you're exemplifying and teaching about the Christian life revolve around Jesus and what he thinks and what his expectations are? Or are you stuck in your own brand of "performance Christianity" that has you feeling frustrated to the point of internally giving up because you just can't keep up the pace?

I'll tell you right now, boys will not and cannot be attracted to a faith that is works oriented. If the Christian you're portraying has to read so many Bible chapters a day, listen to Christian music only, memorize verses, pray eloquent prayers with power, never miss youth group, and go to Christian schools or Christian colleges, then get ready for the wake-up call of your son leaving the church after high school like seventy-five percent of his churchgoing buddies. (And in some denominations the percentage is even higher than that.)

They're leaving in droves, some never to return, because they are not being taught how to reconcile the ideal with the real. They have a performance-driven faith, not one driven by Jesus and his mercy.

So the first thing that must be taught is the reality of Jesus Christ and what he really expects. In the context of all the important spiritual disciplines you want to teach your son during the preteen years, please keep this first and foremost in your mind. Let's start with the Bible.

A Book or a Person?

When you spend time in the Bible, are you spending time with a holy book written by a bad-guy lawgiver . . . or with Jesus?

It's a subtle thing to recognize for yourself; it's even more subtle and hard to grasp for your young son. If you've grown up in your faith thinking that the Bible is a source for all the rules a Christian needs to live by, your son will likely think the same. To some degree, yes, the Bible is a rule book. That is, it's an owner's manual that gives perfect direction on how to live life. But if you open the Bible looking for rules to obey and not a Person to be loved and enjoyed, it won't take long before that book starts collecting dust.

But if when you crack open the Holy Pages, you're sensing that God is waiting to give you a message for today directly from the throne room of heaven, that he wants to use the minutes you give him to speak words of love to you to keep your focus in the right direction, then you're on your way to giving your son a hunger and thirst for God.

God

Does your son know that real men love God? He won't unless he hears those words—"I love God"—come out of your mouth. If God is a real-life passion for you, you have nothing to worry about. Your boy will believe that God is real, lovable, trustworthy, and possesses all those other essential elements of God's character you want him to know about.

I would often start table prayers with, "Father, we love you today. . . ." When I'd pray with my sons about issues in their lives, I would thank God for his love and I would tell God I loved him. My conversations with my boys about God centered on love. Why? Because God is love (1 John 4:8). Because we are challenged to "love the LORD your God with all your heart and with all your soul and with all your strength" (Deuteronomy 6:5). It's *all* about loving the God we can't see.

And Jesus said of course that if we love him, we'll obey him (John 14:15). So it's not as if I always just made him out to be a big teddy bear. I let my sons know that God has expectations about life and behavior, just as I do as a dad. One of the best little sermons I ever gave to my sons was the talk about the difference between their earthly dad and their heavenly Dad. It really allowed them to see that I'm fraught with imperfections, wrong motives, bad timing, and a tongue that can put them in their place at a moment's whim. But God . . . he's perfect, always has our best in mind, knows just the right time to provide the right medicine (discipline) and blessing, and is *always* speaking words of love to them, no matter what they've done and what evil is in their hearts.

Big difference.

Jesus

I mentioned this in the previous chapter, so I won't belabor the point. But Jesus is God, he did the things God would do, and he's waiting for us in heaven with God right now. It is he who is coming back to get us, as a bridegroom receives his bride. It is he who showed us the true character and plan of God by dying on the cross. He's the center of time, the center of the Bible, the center of my life. My life is hidden with Christ in God (Colossians 3:3).

The Holy Spirit and Other Tough Subjects

The Christian life shouldn't be confusing to your son. Neither should the Trinity, since it is such an essential doctrine of the faith. Yet that third person—the Holy Spirit—can be a bit tough to explain. How he comes into our life and what he's doing each hour inside us, well, can be confusing. Because of the variety of traditions relating to this subject, I'm going to abdicate any strong opinion one way or the other. Suffice it to say, the Holy Spirit is a person who needs some in-depth study from the Scriptures.

Whenever I've hit upon a topic so big and so important, I've always just gone the direct route: open up the Bible together, do a weeklong or monthlong study, and let God reveal the truth of his Word within the context of the whole Bible.

What other subjects could use this direct approach? Baptism, Communion, prayer, the fruit of the Spirit, sin and forgiveness, and Old Covenant law versus New Covenant grace make a good start.

You are likely not a Bible scholar, perhaps not even a former Bible college student, but you have a Bible and maybe a concordance. These, combined with some books that talk about these subjects, should be enough to get you started. The biggest value of making a once- or twice-a-year study of some bigger Bible topic a habit with your son is the discussion that happens between you. Your goal is not so much to teach as it is to discover with your son what the Bible really says.

What will you be doing while all this happens? You'll be giving him the confidence that he can "do the Bible." Something very few boys have. If the truth were admitted, a high percentage of men would agree that the Bible can be an intimidating book to crack open. How much more so for your young son! Yet what knowledge or skill is more important for him than knowing how to understand the Word, feed himself spiritually from it, and then teach others as he grows and matures in his faith?

Honestly, I'm not sure I did all that good a job in this area. I thought my boys would ask more questions if they saw me reading or studying, but they didn't. Osmosis is not a good way for some sons to learn how to do the Bible. It takes a strong measure of intentionality to get it done properly.

Tim LaHaye wrote a book years ago called *How to Study the Bible for Yourself.* This would be a great resource to start with. Either read it by yourself or read it together with your son.

Having said all this about making sure that true teaching of spiritual skills and scriptural concepts happens, what will make an equally strong impression on most boys is if you . . .

Get Caught

Reading the Bible with your son will probably not impress him; his catching you reading the Bible by yourself will. Praying with your son will probably not impress him either; it will be his catching you on your knees before you head out to work. The point is, more is often *caught* than *taught*. Many boys learn best by seeing you in action. It will speak volumes more than you telling them what the action is. That means spiritual disciplines have to be a growing part of your life. If your son never sees you crack open the Bible except during Sunday services, guess what? That's right, you don't have to guess. You already know.

If he sees you turning off *SportsCenter* to read a Christian book or your Bible, that will tell him what Christian men do to pursue God more than pursue the world. If he sees you singing worship songs with your eyes closed, one day you may see him doing the same. (And Dad, there ain't nothing like it.)

If it's unnatural for you to do some of these things, you have to discipline yourself to get by this perceived brick wall. If your son doesn't have a hunger and a thirst for God—if you haven't made a relationship with God taste good—then the world will be sure to fill in the gaps. A love for the Word of God, prayer, and worship will help your son be more sensitive to sin, more discerning in his choices, and more confident in himself. Isn't that what you want? Well, it doesn't just happen because you want it. He has to see you enjoying God, basking in God's grace, free from an addiction to "performance Christianity," and serving in the church by using your gifts.

And this has to be a natural part of your life. He must especially hear you pray for him, the family, and yourself—often! The power of humility he will experience by watching you drop your pride and admit you have needs will cause him to do the same, even though the world will do its part to train him to be proud, self-sufficient, and arrogant.

20. Raising Secure Sons

I didn't grow up in a Christian home. In fact, both my parents were married three times before I was out of high school. I had a lot of uncertainty about myself, life in general, and how the heck I fit into the world. Fortunately, in my first year of college these fears drove me to the Lord. And even more fortunately, there were people God had placed around me who could point me in the right direction. I turned out relatively normal.

But a lot of kids don't, including a lot of kids who grow up in Christian homes. Divorce, a relationally clueless parent (or two), and life catastrophes can derail security even in the most well-adjusted boy.

The "Ultimate" Question

How do we raise secure sons?

First, we must teach them that they can be sure of God's loving character.

We didn't do it too often, but two or three times a year I'd let the boys sleep in on Sunday morning. They knew, however, that it meant Dad would lead church at home. One Sunday I wanted to tackle a big topic: Should God get the blame for every bad thing that happens in the world? I pulled out an old broken watch (though they didn't know it was broken) and smashed it four or five times with a hammer on the floor. Pieces flew everywhere. I could see it in their eyes: *Cool. Dad's getting violent.*

I picked up the broken pieces and said, "Stupid watchmaker. I'm going to take this back to K-Mart and get my money back."

The logic was so ridiculous, even they clued in. "Dad, it's not K-Mart's fault the watch broke. You busted it."

"Yeah, but they sold me the watch and later it got busted. Shouldn't they be held responsible if it ever failed to work as it was intended to?"

"Dad. That's the dumbest thing I ever heard."

Perfect opening.

"When something bad happens in the world, whose fault is it?"

Silence.

"If I got cancer next week or walked in front of a dump truck or drove my car over a cliff, who would you feel like blaming?"

Silence.

"When a war breaks out because a few men want to have control over millions of people, and they kill thousands while they're trying to get it, whose fault is it?"

Silence.

"Your natural thought if I somehow died would be that God caused it. Boys, we live in a world that is not heaven. Heaven is out there someday. But this world is not heaven, so we should not expect it to act like it. Bad things can happen anytime to me, your mom, other people you love, maybe you. And your first reaction may be to somehow pin the blame on God. After all, he's God, so he should make your life a constantly happy place, right? Well, no. In fact, he promises tribulation. He assures us that life is not fair. Even in the Bible, bad things happened to good people.

"Fight that urge to blame God for the bad stuff that comes along, because just as it wasn't K-Mart's fault that the watch was broken, it's not God's fault when something goes haywire in your life or in the world around you. Yes, God knows what's going to happen, but he's not the author of evil or sin. Satan is. Jesus called Satan the prince of this world. Satan has influence over people who don't follow God, and therefore bad things are going to happen . . . sometimes to good people. And because we live in the world, we are not immune to being affected by the sin and choices of other people (not to mention, disease, death, and natural disasters). God doesn't cause drunk drivers to kill little children. Choices by normal humans make bad things happen."

"Yeah, but if God knows what's going to happen and he has all the power in the universe, why can't he do something about it?" one of them asked.

"Great question," I said. "Sometimes God *does* intervene. That's why we pray. There are probably thousands of God's miracles we never see because he's doing them while we're not expecting them. But should God control everything? If I controlled you every waking minute, would you think that I loved you or that I was mean?"

"Mean."

"So in order to be loving, I have to give you freedom to make your own choices. Is that what being a good dad is all about?"

"Well, most of the time."

"God's original plan was that we would be in constant fellowship with him, but because he gave us the freedom to make bad choices, we sinned—we do things, even as Christians, that aren't in God's will. Choices have consequences.

"I say all this because I want you to know that God is a good God who has always wanted nothing but the best for his children, you and me. But we will one day be affected by the bad choices of other people. We may even be affected by our own bad choices. So it's important for you to remember that nothing bad that happens in the world is God's fault."

The reason why it is so important for your son to hear this particular sermon in different ways and at various times as he grows up (or one like it, depending on your theology— and I'm sorry my theology slip is showing so much) is that people turn their backs on God mostly because they can't understand pain and tragedy in light of God's love and power. So when something goes wrong, their first inclination is to blame God. Unless they thoroughly understand the message of this sermon before something bad happens, they could be estranged from God for years because they simply can't reconcile a loving God with bad things that directly affect them.

Nothing else in life will trip up our sons like this one thing. God's character must constantly be taught to them so they're always responding to his true, loving nature, not to circumstances that make life uncomfortable or miserable.

A Great Marriage

The second thing we must do to raise secure sons is to help them feel secure about their parents' marriage.

The prework rush was on. I had to be in the office for an early appointment, and Elaine had to go in early to drive customers to their jobs. Before I knew it, we were in a discussion about our oldest son's curfew that night. I was raised a bit more liberally than my wife, and she thinks eleven o'clock is late for a fourteen-year-old, even for the weekend. Normally, I'd just let her decide, but for some reason I didn't want to lose this argument. So to get my point across, I did something I rarely ever do. I raised my voice.

"It's not a school night, and midnight is not that late to stay out if we know where he is!"

Though she was surprised at my tone, she decided to match it.

"You don't have to deal with them when they're too tired to get up for church the next day; you always leave that to me. If they don't get to bed early, they won't get out of bed in the morning!"

"It's one night, for cryin' out loud. Why can't you loosen up a little?"

Just then eleven-year-old Drew came in. "Would you guys stop yelling!"

Then Troy walked by and called me into his room. "Are you and Mom getting a divorce?"

"What?" I asked. "A divorce? Troy, we're just having a loud discussion. Do you hear us argue like this very often?"

"No."

"Then what makes you think we're headed for divorce court?"

"It's just that I had two friends tell me their parents were splitting up, and I thought you might be next."

"Troy . . . I won't be next."

Since both my parents were married multiple times, I know firsthand the fear and insecurity that comes when parents fight. There may be worse feelings for a preteen boy, but not many. I never heard my dad say those words about my mom and their marriage, and sure enough, when I was twelve, they split. I can honestly say that our little family never truly recovered. My siblings and I graduated from high school with tons of "issues" that could have been checked through the stability of two committed, loving parents.

Next to the trauma of a parent dying, nothing brings more insecurity than the thought that parents might divorce. No, it's not the end of the world if it happens. In some situations it could bring some much-needed peace to a household in constant turmoil. And I'm proof that with the Lord, even mixed-up kids can become stable adults.

But the goal is to never leave your son guessing. He should, if at all possible, count on Mom and Dad staying together forever, through good and not so good. Not only does he need this going into his teenage years, but he needs it to look back on when he is tempted to walk out of his marriage. Chances are, he will be tempted. And if good ol' Dad stuck with it, he can too.

And please don't hear me saying that if you're a single dad or are in your second or third marriage, you're going to raise an insecure son. You have some overcoming to do in his little mind, but it can be done. It's beyond the scope of this book to deal further with this all-important issue, except to point you back to the suggestions already made.

Suffice it to say, the best gift you can give your son is a secure marriage. I've rarely seen a man who has pursued God first and his marriage second raise a son unable to cope with the world. Yes, a lot more intentional dadhood stuff has to be done as well, but if you use these priorities as a foundation as you build your relationship with your boy, you're going to raise a son ready for whatever the world can throw at him.

21. Does Your Son's Rededicator Come with a Lifetime Guarantee?

I love the feeling of a clean slate. Whether it's a new basketball season, a new to-do list on a quiet Monday, a new home with the walls painted and carpets cleaned, a new year, even a new solitaire game on the home computer.

But these aren't the only things a Christian has to look forward to. After nearly thirty years as a follower of Christ, I know I can start over with God anytime I want. I've learned that my "rededicator" comes with a lifetime guarantee.

Does your son know that? Does he really believe it?

With two sons who are now nearly grown up, I've concluded that it was their full-time occupation to make mistakes. Let me illustrate with a common source of confrontation: grades.

One of my boys (I won't say who) made some bad free-time choices on a weekend and didn't study enough. Monday rolled around and he wasn't ready for an important test, so he got a bad grade on it. Combine this with some other questionable choices throughout the term, and he was rewarded with a substandard grade on his report card. Though I've never been a fanatic about grades, a lower-than-expected GPA meant less privileges. When this happened, he would typically whine, "You're not fair" and try a host of other lame manipulative tactics designed to convert his problem of "choices have consequences" to one of parental meanness. Sometimes this was followed by hurt feelings, then a confrontation. Things were said that shouldn't be said, and faster than you can say, "You're grounded for two more weeks," he found himself with less privileges than if he'd gotten a 1.8 GPA.

Finally he catches on that he's not in control, comes back contrite, gets a new start, and begins making better choices. Voilà! He gets more privileges, we see a growing sense of responsibility, he shows signs of maturity . . . then (of course) he starts the process all over again.

This type of tussle is wearing on us dads, but it's absolutely essential to the boy struggling for independence. If it's a boy's job to make mistakes, it's our job to help him get through them and move on to maturity.

Did you catch the key point in this whole process?

He gets a new start.

Without this element he'd be stuck. His conscience couldn't get clear and he'd never have the chance to move ahead and mature. And oddly enough, he'd be delayed in getting to the next round of mistakes he must make.

This process is so predictable, I've been tempted to diagram it out so he can get to the start-over point sooner—and make my life easier. And grades are just one part of his life! Before he hit his teen years, we had to deal with issues like showing disrespect to me and his mother, TV choices, and how he treats his brother.

Making mistakes in the everyday areas of life will typically yield immediate consequences. And if he wants out of the consequence and into privilege again, he needs to start over. To make this process into a lifetime lesson for your son, you must turn the corner from what is seen to what is unseen.

Teaching the Unseen

The greater lesson a Christian dad must teach his son is to respond correctly to God when the consequences don't seem to be immediate. Since future lustful thoughts, envy, swearing, jealousy, cheating, and spiritual disinterest don't often get an immediate hand slap, you have to help your son make the choice to "get clean" on his own.

Just as our own hidden sins must be dealt with and cleansed away, so we must teach our sons what I believe is one of the most freeing Scripture passages in the New Testament. Acts 3:19–20 says, "Repent, then, and turn to God, so that your sins may be wiped out, that times of refreshing may come from the Lord, and that he may send the Christ, who has been appointed for you—even Jesus."

God must be viewed as the father in the story of the prodigal son. He's the Good Shepherd. He's Jesus, who died on the cross and rose from the dead. He's the type of God someone should always want—and always feel—they can come back to.

Yes, God is more than just forgiveness and warm feelings. There is a judgment side in the big picture of things, and our secret and not-so-secret sins often *will* have earthly consequences. But he is always the God who promises times of refreshing if true repentance is offered from a heart that wants truth to reign.

A few years ago I was going a bit fast in a residential area and got caught. "Do you know why I pulled you over?" the officer asked after looking at my license and registration.

"Yes, I think I was going too fast down this hill on this dry pavement because there weren't any other cars around, sir." (I had to at least try to get some understanding.)

"I got you on the gun going forty-eight in a twenty-five. Would you like to come see it?"

"No, I trust you. I was speeding."

After the ticket was written, I turned to my boys and asked if they learned anything. Since they're boys, they hadn't caught much of anything except that I got a ticket. "Boys, when you get caught, tell the truth. As you heard, I tried to get out of it a little, but he was right. I broke the law and I have to pay the consequences: fifty-five dollars."

Later I brought home the spiritual lesson. "Who was the bad guy in that ticket thing?" When they said the cop, I told them they were wrong. I was the one who broke the law. "Boys, you may wonder if God's like a heavenly policeman. He's not, though when we sin, God *always* catches us. Sometimes there are consequences you can see; sometimes you can't see them. Either way it's better just to tell God you messed up and ask him for forgiveness. I've found that most of the time he doesn't give you a ticket if you just admit your mistake."

The point is, try to use illustrations from your own life to let your son know the character of God and the consequences of sin. By holding high the value of admitting what you've done—and getting a clean slate—you help him see that he can always start over with God.

The truth about police officers is, they're there to protect and serve. Most aren't bad, and the world would be a rotten place without them. The truth about God is, he can be trusted to forgive no matter what you've done. That makes him fun to be around. The wall can always be knocked down. His rededicator *does* come with a lifetime guarantee.

22. Most of the Questions Answered

Amid the joys and pleasures that await our boys, there is something that few dads like to talk about: the cold, hard world.

Some boys of course get a dose of this reality before they leave the nest. A divorce or the death of a parent, grandparent, sibling, or friend shatters a once idyllic life and awakens the child to the realization that life is not pain-free, that important questions sometimes take some time before they are answered. It's been a few years since the shootings at Columbine High School in Littleton, Colorado, and while God has certainly redeemed this tragedy to some degree, who can confidently give the whys and wherefores of this senseless act of violence?

How prepared are our sons for the life ahead? If we've taught them how to study to get good grades, how to put the proper spin on a free throw, how to survive in a menial job, and how to play the games necessary to get along at youth group and church but have neglected answering questions they perhaps have not even asked yet, have we really done our job?

It's essential to not wait for your son to ask life's tough questions. By occasionally sitting him down and talking about them, you teach some invaluable lessons:

- Asking questions is a good thing not to be afraid of.
- Asking tough questions doesn't offend God or you.
- There *are* answers to most honest questions.
- You, as the dad, are a good source for honest answers, not only now but during your son's whole life.

So what questions should you and your son be discussing in the preteen and teen years? While my list below is far from comprehensive, I've worked with boys long enough to know that these are some of the ones they struggle with the most. Let's divide them into two categories.

Preteen Questions

"If God is love and Christians are commanded to love their neighbor, why do some Christians do a bad job of loving others?"

"Why does God answer some prayers and not others?"

"Is America a Christian nation?"

"In life, do you really reap what you sow . . . or can you get away with bad stuff sometimes?"

"Why should getting to heaven be our goal?"

"What's the purpose of death?"

"Is the Bible *all* true or just *mostly* true?"

"Why is Jesus the only way to God and heaven?"

"Why do children get cancer?"

"If I can't help but sin, why try not to?"

"If I love something too much—like a friend, parent, sport, car, or possession—will God take it away from me to make sure he's number one?"

"What's the real truth about why people die before their time? Does God need them in heaven, is he just insensitive to our needs down here, or is it something else?"

"Why would God allow a Hitler or Stalin to live on this earth?"

"What does God really think about the Jews ... and what should I think?"

"Can you explain the Trinity to me?"

"Is it ever right to hate someone?"

"Why do girls go to the bathroom in groups?"

Early- and Late-Teen Questions

"I know that premarital sex is a biblical no-no, but what about everything but?"

"If we love each other and are going to get married anyway, why not have sex?"

"Why is it really so important to be a virgin when I get married?"

"Does God love me more than he loves homosexuals?"

"What should I really expect out of life?"

"What should I expect out of the person I marry?" (And you *must* be honest!)

"I want to know God's will for my life, especially concerning my future spouse and future job. I've prayed about it a lot, but why doesn't God make these important decisions more clear?"

"Are charismatic Christians all wrong, partly wrong, or not wrong at all? And if they're not wrong at all, what is it and why shouldn't I know about it?"

"Are Catholics Christians?"

"Most Mormons I know are better people than I am. Why do we believe we're right and they're wrong?"

"After I'm twenty-one, what's the best way to think about alcohol?"

"If our bodies are temples of the Holy Spirit, why are there so many Christians with overweight-to-the-point-of-unhealthy temples?"

"Why does going to a Christian college make me more prepared for life?"

"What's the real reason why I should marry a Christian?"

"How much money is enough?"

"What's more important as I choose a career: happiness or the ability to earn a nice living?"

"Opinions are like belly buttons; everyone has one. How do I know which opinions to listen to and which ones to throw out?"

"Why do guys have only one thing on their minds?"

And naturally, the biggest question of all: "Do I as a dad really have to know all the answers to these questions?"

Well, it all depends on how prepared you want your son to be for life. He's going to think about these tough questions sometime. It's better to have them answered by you in a logical, confident manner than by some secular teacher, a godless (yes, godless) friend, or a disenchanted, immature Christian.

Dads have to become experts in answering questions—tough questions. That's the role we inherit as our once pure children learn the cold, hard facts about the world. If you don't know the answers to these questions, get going! Talk to your pastor or a wise friend and start taking notes. Then make "dates" with your son and begin talking through these tough issues. While not every answer you give will be as logical as those Josh McDowell would give, your son will see that your motives are genuine and will appreciate that you're not afraid to talk about anything. Plus it will spur him on to ask even tougher questions! Won't that be fun?

23. Our Worst Nightmare

The headline read, "Teenager Killed by Truck While Riding Bike."

Whether the accident involves riding a bike, driving a car, walking down a road, or hunting, all parents have read headlines about other people's kids senselessly dying before their time. I've read dozens, and while I inwardly cringe and outwardly shake my head, they don't hit home too hard unless you know the kid.

This time I knew the kid.

He had recently graduated from high school and was the child of a good friend. I arrived at the hospital minutes after my friend had, and witnessed the wails of grief that I knew only meant one thing: the child who was set to begin the adventure of an independent life would never get the chance.

Ten minutes later the attending physicians assured those present that it all happened too fast for there to be any pain—even any knowledge of what was happening. I guess a little comfort is better than none.

This wasn't the first time I'd been present at the moment a parent's worst nightmare plays out. Twelve years previous, a bright-eyed fifteen-year-old I knew came by my door trick-or-treating with his girlfriend's two little brothers. Five minutes later his best friend pounded on my door again, out of breath, telling me that Jason had just been hit by a car. A block away he lay critical in the street. An hour later I watched in stunned silence as the emergency room doctor told the parents that their son had died. A drunk driver had cut short his life.

As the Campus Life director in a small community at the time, I was the family's only religious contact. Performing the memorial service—and the graveside burial—helped me conclude something I hadn't fully realized: this is the worst thing in the world for a parent to endure.

After my most recent reminder I went home and hugged my own boys a little tighter. Through tears and a shaking voice I told them that this fine young man, through no choice of his own, would never know the love of a woman, never hug his own children, never present his parents with grandchildren. And to stop the waterworks, I informed them they weren't to leave the house for the next ten years.

Since I'm the reflective type, I spent the next few weeks wondering what the Lord wanted to teach me. Here are two "reminder lessons" I've come up with so far.

1. I felt the Lord reminding me, *Don't you remember giving these two boys to me when they were born? I do, and what you did was right. Don't take them back. They're in good hands with me.*

   I want my sons to be God's property, but I've noticed that as each day goes by, the desire to keep them for myself grows stronger. My love has become a bit more possessive than when they were smaller. Perhaps even a bit more selfish, since I want the benefits of having grown kids (and grandkids) to make my golden years all the more golden.

Natural and normal feelings, to be sure, but potentially dangerous to my emotional and spiritual health should *my* worst nightmare become a reality.

"Lord, again today I give them back to you.
They're safer in your hands than mine anyway."

2.   There are absolutely no guarantees as to how long children are loaned to you. *Love them and enjoy them each day, Greg. Don't ever take them for granted.*

This lesson is equally as hard. How do you *not* take for granted someone you see every day—especially when it seems that half the time they're making your life miserable?

I'm not sure about the answer yet, but if you're sensing the Lord speaking loudly, hear this: spend your time and money on good memories so if anything does happen, you won't have anything to regret.

"Lord, help me to keep my daily priorities in line
with the things that matter most."

It's emotionally unhealthy to constantly think about our worst nightmare, but I've discovered it's good for you—and your son—to be reminded of lessons too important to ignore. Now, before John comes back to give you one more thought from Scripture, put down this book for a second and go hug your boy as tight as you can.

24. A Dad for All Seasons

This is John back again.

If there is one passage of Scripture that has guided my parenting style, it's 1 Thessalonians 5:14. It's not strictly a "parent verse" but it sure could be.

> We urge you, brothers, *warn* those who are idle, *encourage* the timid, *help* the weak, be *patient* with everyone.

Those four words (italics added by me) describe exactly what a dad does throughout his parenting years, which—in case you don't know—is your *whole life!*

Greg's story in the previous chapter reminded me that during their lives our children go through a variety of seasons, in which they need different things from us. Besides losing a grandparent or two, my girls haven't faced loss in the first person (knowing someone their own age who was there one day but gone the next). When that happens, I have to be ready to be what I talked about at the beginning of the book: the dad who is there at the right time in the right way.

In case you haven't caught it yet, what we do as dads isn't just for the benefit of our lives or our sons' lives. What we do—and how we do it—to warn, encourage, and help, all with patience, may reverberate throughout generations.

We're teaching our sons lifetime skills and behaviors (good and bad) that they will hand down to their sons, who just may hand them down to our future great-grandsons! It's an awesome task we have as dads, and one in which we don't get many second chances to succeed.

Throughout this eight- to twelve-year-old age range, your boy will likely face situations that will call upon you to be a dad for all seasons.

At some time in his life your son may be lazy or undisciplined, or "idle," as the Scripture says. He may be idle in his studies, his work, his own parenting, or his faith. If your relationship with him is strong, you'll be there to admonish him to get off his duff and do the right thing. And because you're now convinced that you need to be a student of your son's personality (right, Dad?), you'll know exactly how to do it, as a good dad and life coach should.

At other times in your son's life he'll have that deer-in-the-headlights look of fear in his eyes. He'll be "timid." You've likely been there yourself. An experience with a coach or boss or friend has made you conclude, "What's the use?" And because of this attitude, you chose not to try something that would have brought you great satisfaction. You played it safe. You disobeyed the wise quote from the famous old beer commercial, "You only go around once in life. Go for the gusto." In these days before the Lord's return—whenever that will be—we should be dads who encourage our sons to take a few chances in life. I heard this quote a while back and it's stuck with me: "Something ventured, something gained." Enough said.

At still other times your son is going to be hanging on to the last strand of a long rope, afraid he'll fall. But he won't fall, will he, Dad? Why? Because, Lord willing, your strong arms will not only catch him but lift him to the height necessary to grab the rope with two hands again. His girl will leave him, he'll lose his job, a short bout with depression may hit, or, God forbid, a deep moral or personal failure may cripple his ability to experience God's love. Who's going to be there for him? Who's going to be "Jesus with skin on" when he needs it most? I know who. You, Dad. You'll be there to help.

And through it all, through every stinking mistake he makes, through every financial crisis, through every unkind thing his immature lips utter, through every forgotten thank-you he should have said to you, through every trial he faces in the years ahead, you're going to be the model of patience. Why? Because you're a man who knows his weaknesses, knows that men can't make it alone, and knows that without the patience of God in your life, you would crumple on that scrap heap of male pride that has swallowed so many millions of others.

Memorize this verse as a favor to Greg and me. Then live it out with your son so you can participate with God in raising the next generation of Christian men who will lead their families—and lead the church—to even greater heights than did our generation.

And that's our prayer for you.

"Lord, let it be so."

Part Six:

What-If Games

25. *Games to Grow On*

My (Greg's) boys loved what-if games during their grade school years. The games got them thinking, got them talking, and allowed them to come to answers instead of hearing me sermonize on an important topic. And if they came up with an answer, they owned it.

There are several ways to teach important truths you want your son to carry with him the rest of his life. I was able to spot teachable moments and was a pretty consistent model, but doing something intentionally spiritual—especially during the grade school years—was always more difficult. What-if games allowed my boys to use their imagination. All I did was think back on my grade school days and go through situations they could relate to.

As you read these what-if situations to your boy—or come up with others on your own—the goal is to do it in such a way that he sees himself in the situation. Honest responses are the key, so his answers should never be judged or criticized. After each situation, I've included some questions that will allow your son to think a bit more deeply (and if the question starts with "Dad," that means it's for you!). I've also added Scripture passages so your son can see that God's Word is relevant, even for someone his age. Above all, avoid preaching. You're heading into those years when you're going to want all the honesty you can get from him. The grade school years are a good time to convince your son you can listen to him and accept what he says. (This skill will definitely come in handy later.)

Remember, the goal isn't just to get the right answer; it's to get an honest answer.

Glistening in the Sun: A Lesson in Honesty

What If . . .   Recess is your favorite time of day. You can't wait to get out and run around.

While playing soccer at the morning recess, out on the big sawdust field you spot something glistening in the sun. You walk over, look down, and what do you know, it's a . . .

No, it's not a quarter, it's a gold one-dollar coin! Wow, you don't see many of them these days. You're sure it must be part of some kid's lunch money.

Your friends gather around you, call you lucky, and then tell you to get back in the game. Nobody mentions turning it in at the office. They all expect you to keep it.

You put it in your pocket and keep playing. But meanwhile a bunch of things are going through your head: *Is some kid going to have to skip lunch today? What if it was from a week ago? What would I want someone to do if it were my money?*

As recess ends and you head back inside, that one-dollar gold coin feels pretty good in your pocket.

A Few Questions

What's your first reaction about what you should do with the gold coin?

What would you want someone else to do if it were you who lost the money?

Is this a test or a gift? Did God give the money to you, or did he allow you to find it so you'd wonder what's right to do?

What do you think the reward would be for turning it in? (After he says, "Money," say, "Besides money.")

A Word from the Word

You shall not steal.
> Exodus 20:15

He who has been stealing must steal no longer.
> Ephesians 4:28

Sticks and Stones: A Lesson in Put-Downs

What If . . . Your Sunday school class is planning a Saturday hike up in the mountains. Though you don't know the kids in your class very well, you are looking forward to it. Neither your mom or your dad can go, so it' sort of a day to be on your own.

Arriving at the church to board the bus, you look for someone to buddy up with. You know the names of most of the kids, but you haven't really spent much time with them outside of class.

Three older kids whom you normally get along with get on the bus last, so you follow them, hoping you can sit next to them. They head for the back of the bus and sprawl out on the backseat as if they are going to take a nap.

"Can I sit with you guys?" you ask.

"I don't know if there's enough room. Hey, where'd you get that shirt?" one of the guys asks.

"I think my mom got it at the Christian bookstore."

"Hey, guys, what do you think of someone who wears a shirt that says, 'Lord's Gym' on it?"

"And I suppose your mom cut your hair too?" another says. "It looks like she just put a bowl over your head and snipped away."

Hmmm. You didn't expect these guys to say stuff like this. Maybe they're having a bad day.

"Hey, let the guy sit down," one of the adult leaders says.

As you sit, you're suddenly getting a bad feeling about this. You think you probably should have taken one of the open seats at the front of the bus. As the ride progresses, your feelings turn out to be right. For the rest of the forty-five-minute trip, the guys don't let up. Every time you open your mouth to defend yourself, they find something else to put you down about. Needless to say, it's a very long trip.

A Few Questions

Have you ever been put down before? How did it make you feel?

Have you ever put someone else down? Why? Did you think about how it was making that person feel?

How would you handle a situation like this?

Dad: Why do you think people put down others? What are they trying to accomplish?

A Word from the Word

Better a patient man than a warrior, a man who controls his temper than one who takes a city.

Proverbs 16:32

A man's wisdom gives him patience; it is to his glory to overlook an offense.

Proverbs 19:11

Quick Glances: A Lesson in Cheating

What If . . .   It's Thursday. One more school day until the weekend! Suddenly the teacher announces a pop quiz that you haven't studied for.

A quiz! you think. Since you haven't even looked at your books, you know there's no way you'll do well. The guy next to you pulls out some paper and says, "I have this one aced. I've been studying all week." He's the smartest kid in class. He aces *every* test.

You pull out your paper and pencil, listening carefully as the teacher reads off the first question. When your neighbor starts writing, your eyes take a quick glance at his paper. The guy finishes writing down his answer before you can even think of one.

As the teacher reads the second question, you know this test is going to get ugly unless you think quickly.

A Few Questions

What would you do if the teacher turned her back?

What would most of your classmates do in this situation?

If you knew you wouldn't get caught, would you look at his paper . . . just this once?

Dad: What would you want your son to do in this situation? Why?

Dad: What would you have done in the same situation when you were in school?

A Word from the Word

The LORD abhors dishonest scales, but accurate weights are his delight.

Proverbs 11:1

Blessed are they who maintain justice, who constantly do what is right.

Psalm 106:3

Odd Man Out?: A Lesson in Loyalty

What If . . .   You have three buddies with whom you spend all your time at school—and afterward. The whole school year you've been inseparable. Whenever you're on the playground at recess, all four of you are doing something: soccer, football, swinging from the monkey bars, making up imaginary games, all sorts of stuff.

As you're heading home from school one day with two of these friends, they start talking about the other guy, who isn't there.

"He's getting to be a real dweeb," says one.

"I know. He's saying stupid stuff to girls, and all he talks about is sports," says the other.

"Who are you talking about?" you ask.

"Tim, of course. Haven't you been listening to all the dumb stuff he's been saying lately?"

"No. Like what?" you question.

"Like talking about girls all the time and wanting to go chase them. He even said we should call up girls and hang up on them. He's a jerk."

"Plus he thinks he's really hot in sports. We've talked it over. What do you think? Is it time to get rid of him?"

"You mean, just ignore him, like he's not even there? Not call him anymore or go over to his house?"

"Yeah," they both say at the same time.

"Wait a minute. Tim's been our friend for a long time. Have you even talked to him about what he's doing?"

"Well . . ."

"I say we need to give the guy a chance. Maybe we can all talk to him and tell him where he's messing up. I think he'll listen."

"I don't. He's too stuck on himself. I say let's leave him in the dust."

"I can't believe you guys are thinking this way," you say. "Doesn't the guy deserve a second chance? Wouldn't you want to be told something if you were the one acting weird?"

"Maybe, but it's too late. I can hardly even stand being around the guy."

"And maybe *you* need to decide what group you're going to be in."

"Maybe I do."

A Few Questions

Have you ever had to choose between friends? What did you do?

How important is loyalty in a friendship?

If you were the guy the other kids were talking about, what would you want them to do: tell you how they feel or just ignore you?

Can you remember a time when the friends of Jesus had to choose between loyalty to him or loyalty to the world?

A Word from the Word

A friend loves at all times, and a brother is born for adversity.
Proverbs 17:17

A man of many companions may come to ruin, but there is a
friend who sticks closer than a brother.
Proverbs 18:24

Avoiding the Root of All Evil: A Lesson in Greed

What If . . .   To get you to do things, your parents have to
motivate you properly. And what motivates you the most
(much of the time) is money.

During the summer, to get you to read a book, they pay
you a dollar or two (depending on how thick it is). During the
school year, whenever you get an A in a class, they give you
three dollars! And then of course the whole year through, you
don't get your allowance until you do your chores.

Plus you are always trying to do extra work for more
money. If the cars need washing and vacuuming, you nego-
tiate with your dad or your mom about how much you
should get if you do the work. Ditto with raking leaves,
sweeping, dusting, and so on.

It's not that you are an absolute greed freak; it's just, well,
you like to have money to spend. And what do you spend it
on? Posters, sports cards, candy, clothes, sometimes presents
for others. At least three or four times a week you can be
found in your room counting your money.

A Few Questions

Do you think it would be unusual for a family or a kid to
do this?

Would you say the kid is greedy, or is he just learning to appreciate having money?

We know that money isn't evil but the love of money is. Has the love of a possession ever caused you to tune out other things that are important in life?

Dad: How tempting is it for you to put possessions above other priorities? How do you fight that temptation?

A Word from the Word

No one can serve two masters. Either he will hate the one and love the other, or he will be devoted to the one and despise the other. You cannot serve both God and Money.

Matthew 6:24

The love of money is a root of all kinds of evil. Some people, eager for money, have wandered from the faith and pierced themselves with many griefs.

1 Timothy 6:10

Star Shooter: A Lesson in Humility

What If . . . You're a basketball player for the school's sixth-grade team. Your team is pretty good and you get to play a lot. The reason: You're a good passer and the coach likes having guards who can get the ball to the big guys. You don't shoot a lot—unless you're wide open. Quite a few fans show up to your games.

This game has been a tough one. Your opponents are trying everything to win, even leaving some of their weaker players on the bench so the regulars can get more time. Though your coach wants to beat the other coach, he doesn't stoop to making players ride the pines just to get a win—usually.

The buzzer ends the third quarter and your team is down by six. Things definitely don't look good. Your coach takes you and a few other starters out and puts in the second-stringers—just like always. Two minutes later your team is down by ten! It looks as if there's no hope. At the next whistle a minute later, however, the coach puts the regulars back in. It's a little early for that, but you sense he wants to see if you can make a comeback.

As soon as you go in, you steal the ball and go all the way for a layup. The next time down they take a shot and miss. Bringing the ball up court, you spot one of your best shooters in the corner at the three-point line. You fire him a perfect pass, he sets, shoots . . . swish! Down by five with three minutes to go.

The other team takes it down court quickly and gets an easy layup. Down seven again. One of the other guards brings the ball up court and sees you breaking for the basket. He gives you a bounce pass and you stop and pop. It hits the glass and goes in. Down five.

They inbound the ball and you steal it again. As you head toward the basket, the guy from the other team who threw the bad pass comes hard at you. You take one dribble to your right and lay it in just as he hacks your arm. You sink the free throw and your team is only down by two with a minute and a half left. That's when the other team tries to stall. They're passing the ball around without trying to score. Your team is playing good defense, though, and you know your opponents can't hold on to the ball forever. Finally one of their players panics and takes a bad shot.

With fifteen seconds left, you're dribbling the ball up court, looking for your three-point shooter. He's covered. Dribbling to your left, you lob the ball to the center, hoping he can make a move and get an easy shot to tie the game. Seven seconds. Immediately three guys cover him, so he kicks the ball back out to you. Glancing at the clock, then the rim, you let the ball fly from behind the three-point line. It hits the back of the rim ... goes straight up in the air ... and through the net. A three-pointer! Your team wins by one!

In case you weren't counting, you scored ten points and had one assist in the last four minutes! Everyone runs up to you to give you high fives. The coach gives you a big hug and lifts you off the ground. Mom and Dad are clapping and screaming like high schoolers.

The next day in school everyone has heard about how great a game you played and comes up to congratulate you.

A Few Questions

There's nothing wrong with playing well and being congratulated. But sometimes too much attention over something good a person has done can give him a big head. How are you going to deal with all the attention?

What do you think pride is? Can you have too much of it?

What could you do to try to stay (not just act) humble?

Feeling good about your accomplishments is important, but have you ever known someone who makes sure everyone recognizes him after he does something good? What do you think of such a person?

Dad: What's the best way to keep yourself from becoming too proud?

A Word from the Word

Let another praise you, and not your own mouth; someone else, and not your own lips.
Proverbs 27:2

Do not think of yourself more highly than you ought, but rather think of yourself with sober judgment, in accordance with the measure of faith God has given you.
Romans 12:3

An Hour Late and Five Dollars Short: A Lesson in Responsibility

What If . . .   It's Saturday morning—allowance day!

For five dollars a week, all you have to do is take out the garbage, empty the dishwasher, fold a few clothes, sweep the garage, do a little yard work, and keep your room clean. Not a bad deal, considering that your parents could choose to not give you anything. They could decide that being part of the family means you do certain things whether you get paid or not. But they don't. They cough it up every week, just like clockwork.

This particular Saturday you're lying around watching TV when the phone rings. It's your best friend, Chuck. He asks you if you want to go see a movie with him and his family today. You check with your mom and she says that would be fine.

"She said yes," you tell Chuck. "What time will you be by to pick me up?"

"Noon," he says. "See you then."

You race to your room to check the cash supply. You can only find a dollar in change. *Gotta quit buying that candy after school*, you think.

Hey! It's Saturday. That means your dad owes you five dollars!

But when you find him, he says he'd love to give you the money but you haven't done your chores yet. Checking the clock, you see that it's a quarter past eleven. You've only got forty-five minutes to do all your chores! Yikes! *Why did I lie around so much this morning!*

You're nearly certain that you can't get your chores done in that amount of time, so you plead your case with Dad.

"I promise that as soon as I get home from the movie, I'll get everything done. I'll even do some extra stuff for free."

"I know that seems like a good offer to you, Son," he says, "but that's not the deal. We agreed that you would do your chores, and then I'd give you the money. It's been like pulling teeth to get you to do them on time for the last three months. How do I know you'll actually do them? Your little brother has even tried to pick up the slack for you by filling in. I'm sorry, but the only choice I have is to stick to my guns. You have to learn how to be responsible, so you may as well learn now. If you have them done, you'll get your five dollars. Not before. Not this time."

You hang your head as you walk away without saying a word.

A Few Questions

Would you get busy doing your chores, or would you just think they couldn't get done, so why hurry?

When you show you're responsible in the little things, your parents learn to trust you with other—oftentimes bigger—things. Is this a fair way to determine if you're ready to be trusted with other, more adult-type activities?

How would you react if you were twenty minutes away from getting your chores done, your friends came by to pick you up, and your dad still wouldn't budge, so you had to tell them you couldn't go?

Dad: Talk about what you believe about the importance of your child learning responsibility.

A Word from the Word

The plans of the diligent lead to profit as surely as haste leads to poverty.

Proverbs 21:5

The sluggard craves and gets nothing, but the desires of the diligent are fully satisfied.

Proverbs 13:4

A Hurting Friend: A Lesson in Real Friendship

What If . . .   It's a Monday afternoon and you're riding your bike home from school. You had to take care of a few things after classes, so it was nearly four thirty before you set out. The clouds are getting thicker and it's starting to get dark, but you know you have plenty of time to get home.

You live in a suburb close to the city. About every subdivision has a large brick wall surrounding it. Lately you've noticed a lot more graffiti on the walls than normal. You wonder if some gangs are moving into the area.

As you pass the back side of one group of homes, you see a guy next to one of the walls. He pulls something out of a bag and then starts spray painting some words. Stopping, you look hard to see what he's writing. Then the figure turns around and glances in your direction. He looks familiar!

Getting back on your bike, you ride closer, but real slowly. You can't believe it. It's one of your good friends! He spots you and starts running, not knowing who you are. You take off fast on your bike and easily catch up to him. You yell to him that it's you. He turns around to see, then slows down.

"It's just you," he says. "I thought it was someone who would turn me in."

"What are you doing spray painting that wall?" you ask. "If you get caught, you'll just have to clean it up. Plus your parents will probably ground you for a month. What are you thinking?"

"Ah, my parents don't care what I do. Besides, it doesn't look like they're going to be together that much longer anyway. My dad left really mad a couple weeks ago and hasn't been back. I bet they end up divorced."

"What does your mom think?"

"All she does is cry and talk on the phone. We haven't talked much. I think she's avoiding the subject."

"So why are you spray painting the walls? Is someone making you do it?"

"They don't *make* me do anything. They just say it would look cool to see the gang's name on the wall."

"You joined a gang?!"

"Not yet. I'm still being looked at."

A Few Questions

Though you may never find yourself in this situation, what would you do if you had a friend who was doing something this stupid?

Why do you think this guy wants to join a gang?

Should you tell on a friend to make sure he doesn't get into worse trouble? What are the consequences if you do? What are the potential benefits?

Who would you talk with to help you decide what to do?

A Word from the Word

Wounds from a friend can be trusted, but an enemy multiplies kisses.

Proverbs 27:6

Above all, love each other deeply, because love covers over a multitude of sins.

1 Peter 4:8

Not All Fun: A Lesson in Pitching In

What If . . .   "It's going to be a blast," you tell your best friend on the phone. "First we meet at the church with our sleeping bags, pillows, and pack, we load up the vans, then we head out into the wilderness! It only takes about an hour, and when we get there all the leaders cook the food while the kids go exploring. We get to stay up as late as we want, eat s'mores, tell stories . . . you'll love it!"

You're friend is convinced; he's going!

A week later you're at the church, loading up and heading out. Even if it's just an overnighter, it still seems like a week at camp.

After an hour in the van, you pull into the camp. Your friend gives you a look like, *This place is perfect!*

"Okay, let's get our stuff put away and start finding out what's around here," you say.

"Campers! Campers!" the head guy yells, trying to get everyone's attention. "We have a lot of work to do before dinner, so we need everyone to pitch in. You six guys go with Mr. Maxwell. You have the dinner detail. You four (pointing at you, your friend, and two other guys) go with Mr. Abbott and start setting up the tents for the rest of us. It should take you until dinnertime. You seven guys go find as much firewood as you can. We'll need it pretty soon 'cause it's getting dark. Okay, guys, let's get it done."

Your friend gives you that *I thought this was going to be a vacation* look.

"It wasn't like this last year," you say. "Last year the adults did everything and we just ran around."

Mr. Abbott overhears what you've said. "Yeah, but that wasn't any fun. You guys didn't learn anything. This year we're a team. And everyone's important. We all have to help if we're going to get things done. Let's get to work."

Work?

A Few Questions

How would you feel about having to pitch in and help get the camp ready?

Do you pitch in at home to help around the house and yard?

How is a family like a team? What would happen if one of the teammates didn't do his or her job?

When you are asked to do things around the house, what is your first reaction? How could that get better?

A Word from the Word

Even when we were with you, we gave you this rule: "If a man will not work, he shall not eat." We hear that some among you are idle. They are not busy; they are busybodies. Such people we command and urge in the Lord Jesus Christ to settle down and earn the bread they eat.

2 Thessalonians 3:10–12

Phone Answers: A Lesson in Homework

What If . . .   You're a pretty good student in almost every subject—except math. When it comes to having the desire to get homework done in that subject, well, let's just say you'd rather do anything but that.

Unfortunately, you can never get out of it. You've begged your dad to help you with it, secretly hoping he would just tell you the answers (which he did sometimes). Even Mom has been a help when you were stuck. But now they say they'll help you with the answers but you have to do the work yourself.

Panic sets in. Your brain just doesn't understand math. You're afraid that if you don't do well on the homework, your parents will withhold the three dollars they promised to give you for every A or B you get on your report card.

All of a sudden it comes to you.

I'll call Jerod and tell him I'm just checking my answers with his, you think. *I'll ask what he got, then say, "That's what I got."*

A brilliant plan indeed. In fact, it works the first few nights. Jerod doesn't catch on to what you're doing. But your parents do. Every night after dinner you've been escaping to their room to use the phone in private. Unfortunately, you forgot how funny it might look if you took your homework in there with you. After a few more days your dad comes into your room before bedtime.

"Son, why are you taking your math homework into our bedroom with you every night when you say you're going to use the phone? You haven't been asking us for help on it lately. How are you doing in class?"

A Few Questions

> You've just been busted, but there is probably a way to skirt the truth so as not to lie but not to tell your father the truth. What would you do?

> Do you feel pressured by your parents in any way to get great grades?

> Is getting good grades more important than not cheating to do it?

A Word from the Word

> Stand firm and hold to the teachings we passed on to you, whether by word of mouth or by letter.
> 2 Thessalonians 2:15

> Pray for us. We are sure that we have a clear conscience and desire to live honorably in every way.
> Hebrews 13:18

Rubbing It In: A Lesson in Sportsmanship

What If . . .   You're playing baseball against a team that you've always considered your arch rival. They're from another grade school in your area, and you know a few of the players. You've grown up playing against them . . . and you don't like them very well. In fact, the parents on both teams don't even like each other.

They've beaten you once already this year in a close game—on their field. The umpire made a few questionable calls that didn't go in your favor. But now you're ahead five to four in the top of the sixth. The other team has their last ups. If you can hold them, you'll win.

The first guy up lines a single to center field, where you field it and throw it to second base. The next guy up hits a grounder up the middle. Your shortstop knocks it down and flips the ball to second base to force the runner there. One out. On four straight pitches, the next guy up walks. Runners on first and second, one out . . . and one of your old "buddies" is up. He's a good hitter. In the last game he hit a double to knock in two runs and seal the win.

He takes a strike and swings at the next. The next two pitches are balls. It's two and two as the runners take their lead. As the pitcher winds up, you see the runners break for second and third—trying a double steal. The batter smacks a line drive in your direction, but you get a good jump on it. Running forward and to your left, you stick your glove out and . . . and . . . make an incredible catch! Keeping your balance, you see that the guy who was on second is all the way to third. The shortstop is on second, waving his arms. You plant your foot and make a perfect throw to second before the runner gets back.

Double play! You win!

Needless to say, you're mobbed by your teammates. Back at the dugout, as you're getting ready to give the other team a yell, you notice they're not going to give you one. Your team does it anyway, then lines up to shake their hands. You can't wait to see the guy whose ball you caught.

A Few Questions

Are you the type who might rub it in somehow, or would you do something else?

When you think of the word *sportsmanship*, what comes to your mind?

Is it ever okay to not be a good sport?

A Word from the Word

He gives us more grace. That is why Scripture says: "God opposes the proud but gives grace to the humble."
James 4:6

Though the LORD is on high, he looks upon the lowly, but the proud he knows from afar.
Psalm 138:6

Dad's Big Helper: A Lesson in Helping Out

What If . . .   It's been a long week for you—and your dad. You've had tons of homework, soccer practices, band rehearsals, church on Wednesday . . . You haven't even watched TV all week!

Your dad, on the other hand, has been swamped beyond anything you can remember. He's off for work before you even get up every morning, and he's not home until you're just about ready to doze off to dreamland. A few coworkers of his are on vacation, and the company has had hundreds more orders than usual, so he's had to fill in. It happens every year, but it's never been this bad.

Finally the week is over. Your dad arrives home about eight thirty on Friday night. This time you're still up. He comes into your room to catch up on the week with you. It's great to talk with him again. He asks you about your week, so you try to recount it as best you can. You ask him about his, and he just gets this weary look on his face. He explains a little of what he's doing and says it doesn't look as if it's going to slow down in the next couple of weeks, either.

Fortunately for you, your schedule *will* slow down! This weekend and next week will be a breeze compared with the last one.

After breakfast on Saturday morning, your mom gives you a note from your dad. Here's what it says:

> *Good Morning! Sorry to just leave a note, but I had to head to work early again. I really need your help this week around the house, especially in the yard. Mom's got a hectic week, so I'd like you to take care of these things: weed the garden and the flower beds, sweep the garage, wash the cars and hose down the driveway, straighten up my workbench, and get the toy area all in order. I know that's a lot, but with me being gone so much, I need you to pitch in. Thanks.*
>
>

Love,

Dad

Wow! That's a lot of work!

A Few Questions

What would you do if your dad gave you that big an assignment?

How do you feel about pitching in around the house?

Growing up has a lot of benefits, but it also means accepting more responsibility. How do you think you'll respond when you have to become even more responsible?

A Word from the Word

Don't let anyone look down on you because you are young, but set an example for the believers in speech, in life, in love, in faith and in purity.

1 Timothy 4:12

Do you see a man skilled in his work? He will serve before kings; he will not serve before obscure men.

Proverbs 22:29

The Vicious Loudmouth: A Lesson in Revenge

What If . . .   Every Wednesday night you go to a group at your church called Kids' Club. You play games, memorize verses, and work your way through a Kids' Club handbook that has a lot of Bible stuff in it. The leaders work pretty hard at making it fun for all the kids—and most of the time it is fun.

Except there is this one kid named Shaun who drives you crazy. It's as if he has to be the center of attention. He thinks he's Mr. Comedian and is always cutting other people down. During the discussion portion of class, you raise your hand to answer a question. You don't give the right answer and that's when Shaun starts in on you. Before the teacher has stopped him, he's nailed you good—twice! The class erupts in laughter and you feel really stupid.

After Kids' Club is over, you stay to talk to the leader about the upcoming day hike. Your dad said he would drive, and you need to get a few more details for him. As you're heading out the door, the teacher notices that Shaun has left his backpack. He asks if you'd mind trying to catch him in the parking lot.

Swinging the backpack over your shoulder, you race up the stairs toward the parking lot to see if you can catch Shaun before he leaves. A few thoughts run through your head about what you'd really like to do with the backpack, but you push them from your mind.

You head out into the parking lot in the pouring rain to see if you can find Shaun. After a few minutes of looking into car windows, you conclude that he is gone. Now you're really mad. Not only did the guy make you look like a fool in class, but you're soaking wet too.

What do I do now with the backpack? you think. *Hmmm. I could "accidentally" leave it out in the rain.*

A Few Questions

Would you be tempted to take revenge on Shaun?

When someone does something to you that makes you look or feel bad, do you try to get him back?

Does getting someone back really make you feel better?

A Word from the Word

Love your enemies, do good to those who hate you, bless those who curse you, pray for those who mistreat you.
Luke 6:27–28

Do not take revenge, my friends, but leave room for God's wrath, for it is written: "It is mine to avenge; I will repay," says the Lord.

Romans 12:19

Light-Fingered Friends: A Lesson in Stealing

What If ...   It's a Saturday afternoon and you're on your way to the store with a few of the guys in the neighborhood. You know them pretty well because you've been playing with them for years. Most don't go to church, but for the most part they're good friends.

When you hit the store, you go straight to the ice cream section. You have $1.80 in your pocket and you think you'll have enough for a Dove Bar. The other guys fan out throughout the store in search of whatever goodies they want.

As you're standing in line, a couple of the guys just go right through without buying anything. They motion for you to come with them but you have to pay for your ice cream. They motion again but you point to the Dove Bar and wait your turn.

As you get to the front of the line, you see another of your buddies going past the registers without buying anything.

That's weird, you think, *looks like I'm going to be the only one with something to eat. I suppose I'll have to share.*

When you get outside, the guys are down by the corner of the store. Walking closer to them, you see they're munching away on candy bars.

"Where'd you guys get that stuff?" you ask.

"From the nice folks at the store, of course," one says. "We tried to get you out of there so you wouldn't have to waste your money, but you were clueless."

"Clueless about what? Did you guys steal that stuff?"

"Hey, with such poor security, they deserve to have stuff stolen from them. That was the easiest store I've ever stole from."

You're having a tough time believing that these guys actually stole that candy, but the truth of it is being stuffed into their faces.

"Here, take a Reeses," one of them says, offering you one of your favorite candy bars.

A Few Questions

Knowing that was a stolen candy bar, what would you do or say?

When are you most tempted to take something that doesn't belong to you?

What do you think should be the consequences if you steal?

Dad: When you were your son's age, did you ever steal anything? Did you get caught? What happened?

A Word from the Word

He who conceals his sins does not prosper, but whoever confesses and renounces them finds mercy.
Proverbs 28:13

Ill-gotten treasures are of no value, but righteousness delivers from death.
Proverbs 10:2

The Tough Guy: A Lesson in Gloating

What If . . . Since kindergarten, soccer has been your sport. You haven't missed a season, fall or spring. Playing competitively, you know soccer as well as anyone your age. You know the positions, you know the penalties, you know how to hit the far goal post, you know the game.

One thing you've also learned is how to play in a controlled, aggressive way. That is, the contact you initiate—most of the time—is legal and fair. Other kids who play at your level know almost as much as you.

At a tournament in another town, you're playing against a team you've never played against before. As a right-winger, your job is to be one of the first players to push up when the ball crosses midfield. The guy who is marking you is a little bigger than you—and he's rough. On a couple of plays early in the game, he put a hard check on you to steal the ball and move it the other way. You looked at the ref for a call but it never came. At halftime the score was still zero to zero.

The second half begins and you're taking the ball down the side. The same guy moves up on you and rams you right to the ground. Finally the whistle blows. The ref calls the other kid over and talks to him. Then he pulls out his yellow card and raises it in the air.

That will keep him off me for a while, you think. *He's got to back off and play fair now.* And he does . . . for about another ten minutes. That's when your team scores. In this game, with your defense playing so well, that could be the game winner.

With the momentum on your side, the defense controls the ball and moves it to your side of the field. As you're racing down the sideline, you see the guy coming for you again, so you stop the ball and dribble it to the middle. This catches him off guard, but he quickly recovers and starts for you again—this time from behind. Just as you enter the goal box, the guy puts a hard trip on you from behind. Quickly the ref blows his whistle, calls the other player over, and gives him a red card! Not only is he out of the game, but this eliminates him from the next game in the tournament too.

The coach lets you take the penalty shot and you put it in. The games ends; you've won two to nothing.

After the game it's customary for each team to line up and shake hands at the center of the field. As the guy passes you by, you have a choice as to what you'll say or do.

A Few Questions

What would you feel like doing?

What do you think the word *gloat* means?

When you beat someone, whether it's in a sport or a game, do you like to rub it in?

Dad: What do you think is the correct way to win gracefully?

A Word from the Word

You should not look down on your brother
    in the day of his misfortune,
nor rejoice over the people of Judah
    in the day of their destruction,
nor boast so much
    in the day of their trouble.

Obadiah 12

When I stumbled, they gathered in glee; attackers gathered against me when I was unaware. They slandered me without ceasing.

Psalm 35:15

The Captain's Tough Choice: A Lesson in Love

What If . . .   It's lunch recess again, so it's time for everyone to line up and be selected for the football game. The routine is always the same: everyone stands in line while the two captains pick their teams. Every day it's the same thing. Since you're a pretty good football player, you're always one of the first few to be picked. No one ever seems to complain but you've wondered how Mike feels. He's the guy who's always picked last.

One day the guys who normally pick teams aren't around, so you're told to go out and pick. You've never had this chance before. Suddenly you know how it feels to be a captain. You want to have a good team so you can win.

Your first two picks are your best friends, while the other guy picks two good players. You can see where this is leading. Ol' Mike is going to be picked last again unless you break with tradition. You could surprise everyone by picking him third, but then you'd be stuck with a guy who can't throw the ball and can barely catch.

A Few Questions

What would you do?

How do you think it would make Mike feel if for once he wasn't picked last? How would you feel if you were always the last one picked?

How important is it for you to win at lunchtime football? Does anyone really care who wins and loses?

Though you probably know what Jesus would do, why is it so hard to do that?

A Word from the Word

As God's chosen people, holy and dearly loved, clothe your-selves with compassion, kindness, humility, gentleness and patience.

Colossians 3:12

Each of you should look not only to your own interests, but also to the interests of others.

Philippians 2:4

How Much Does Friendliness Cost?: A Lesson in Loving the Unlovely

What If . . .   As one of the more friendly kids at school, you have lots of friends. Nearly every week someone calls and asks you to come over to play. You of course do. Basket-ball, soccer, baseball, sports cards—whatever your friends want to do, you'll join in.

Naturally, you have four or five friends who are closer than all the rest. These are kids you'll spend the night with or who will spend the night with you. Then there's the friends at church. They're not quite as close, because you don't spend as much time with them, but they're good guys.

One day while climbing the monkey bars at recess, a kid comes over to where you and the other guys are showing off to the girls. He tries to join in. Now this guy is not one of your close friends. In fact, you've hardly even talked to him since school started. He hasn't learned how to fit in with the rest of the guys yet, he doesn't talk too much, and he isn't into sports (and he is usually the last guy picked for football at lunchtime recess).

The guy is nice but sometimes he tries a little too hard. While everyone is goofing off, he asks you if you can come over to his house after school the next day. All your friends look at you, then at him, then back at you.

Thinking quickly, you say you'll check with your mom and tell him tomorrow. You can almost predict that if you go over to his house, it'll be boring because you don't have a lot in common. Plus you're not sure you want him to start thinking of you as one of his friends.

You ask your mother and she says, "Fine with me."

Now you're faced with a dilemma: go over to the guy's house or somehow (without lying) let him know you don't want to.

A Few Questions

What would you do and why?

Are most kids who are loners weird, or have they just never been given a chance?

What would be the consequences of going to this person's house? How about the benefits?

There are several reasons why some kids don't have many friends: a person may have moved a lot; his parents may never have taught him how to talk to others; he may be afraid of rejection (based on past experience). What can be done to help someone learn how to form friendships?

A Word from the Word

The Son of Man came to seek and to save what was lost.
Luke 19:10

Greater love has no one than this, that he lay down his life
for his friends.
John 15:13

Early Riser: A Lesson in Spending Time with God

What If . . .   Getting up and ready for school has always
been kinda tough. It's not that you stay up late, it's just that
you're not a morning person. When the alarm goes off at
7:15, you sleep right through it. Then when your mom
comes in at 7:20, you wish you could continue sleeping—
but you know you can't.

"Breakfast is in ten minutes," she always says. "If you want
it hot, you'd better get dressed and come on out."

So you lumber out of bed, sleepwalk through putting
your clothes on, and do a dazed shuffle into the kitchen for
some chow.

For some reason, however, on this Thursday morning you
wake up at 6:55—and can't go back to sleep. With your
clothes on in a minute, you walk out and surprise your mom.

"What's for breakfast?" you ask, almost in a chipper tone.

"What are you doing up so early?" she asks in response.

"Couldn't sleep, so I thought I'd just face the world a little earlier. You don't have to make anything today; I'll just
have cereal."

"Sounds fine to me."

Now it's barely 7:30 and you're already dressed and fed.
With no homework to catch up on, all you have to do is

make your bed and brush your teeth. Class doesn't start for an hour. . . . What are you going to do now?

You could read that new book you bought at the book fair. You could go watch a video or some cartoons. Or . . . there's that Bible next to your bed that you never seem to have time for.

A Few Questions

Be honest: what would you do?

How motivated are you to read your Bible at all?

What would it take to help you be more motivated and disciplined to open it up a few times a week?

Dad: Talk about your own Bible reading and prayer habits, good and bad.

A Word from the Word

Jesus often withdrew to lonely places and prayed.
Luke 5:16

Jesus said, "If you remain in me and my words remain in you, ask whatever you wish, and it will be given you."
John 15:7

The Prince Is Powerful: A Lesson about the Prince of Darkness

What If . . .   You've lived next door to Matt since you can remember. You went through kindergarten and most of grade school together. When it came to sports, you guys appeared next to each other in every team picture: baseball, soccer, YMCA basketball, everything.

Sadly, when Matt was in fourth grade, his parents got a divorce. His dad moved out one day and now Matt only sees him about once a month. Matt's mom tried hard to keep family life normal, including going back to work to keep the house. Unfortunately, Matt's dad wasn't too consistent with his child support payments, so they eventually had to sell their home and move to an apartment.

Matt still goes to the same school you go to, so you see him every day, but you've noticed he's changed. He brings these scary, horror-type books to school all the time and reads them at recess and lunch. He doesn't play soccer anymore with the rest of the guys the way he used to; he mainly keeps to himself. When he does talk, it's always about the latest book he read or another slasher movie he saw at his dad's house while watching HBO.

To try to see what's going on, you invite him to your birthday sleepover with a few other guys on a Friday night. When he gets there, he has this big backpack and a sleeping bag.

"Have I got a game for us later, after your parents go to bed," he says.

Matt seems agitated the whole time he's at your house; he even reads while the rest of the guys and you go play football. About eleven o'clock, after your parents have gone to bed (with instructions that lights-out will be 1:00 a.m.—if everything is quiet), he pulls out this thing called a Ouija board. He starts explaining how it works, turns out the lights, and turns on a flashlight.

Before he can get started, your dad comes down. When he sees what's going on, he puts the board back in the box and says Matt can take it with him in the morning. Then he says, "Lights out."

A Few Questions

Matt has filled his mind with some pretty bad stuff since his dad left. Who do you think he is being influenced by?

When you're in grade school, you rarely see Satan working behind the scenes to ruin someone's life. As you get older, it becomes more obvious. What do you know about Satan?

Dad: Explain that though it's not good to dwell on Satan, it is a good idea to know how he works. Talk about how his influence starts in the mind and then works its way to behavior.

Dad: What else do you know about Satan's plans for humans, God's unique creation?

A Word from the Word

Be self-controlled and alert. Your enemy the devil prowls around like a roaring lion looking for someone to devour.
1 Peter 5:8

The Lord will rescue me from every evil attack and will bring me safely to his heavenly kingdom.
2 Timothy 4:18

About the Authors

Greg Johnson is a 1979 graduate of Northwest Christian College in Eugene, Oregon, where he earned two bachelor degrees, in biblical studies and psychology. He worked for ten years at Campus Life, a division of Youth for Christ, in Eugene and Seattle before joining Focus on the Family as the founding editor of their teen boys' magazine, *Breakaway*. After writing thirteen books for teens and eight other books (devotional/marriage/family), in 1994 he joined Alive Communications, where he serves as vice president. He has been married for twenty-seven years to Elaine, his high school sweetheart. They have two sons, Troy, twenty, and Drew, eighteen, and reside in Colorado Springs.

John Trent, Ph.D., is president of StrongFamilies.com. He has authored or coauthored more than a dozen award-winning and best-selling books, in addition to writing five books for children. He teaches conferences, speaks at Promise Keepers conferences, and has been a featured guest on numerous radio and television programs. John and his wife, Cindy, have two daughters, Kari and Laura, and live in Scottsdale, Arizona.

If you have a comment about the content of this book or perhaps have stories or ideas from your life as a dad that have been successful in moving your son to Christian manhood, please email Greg at gigariter7@aol.com.